The Switch: The Secret Law of Attraction

By Craig Beck

Forward

Make no mistake this book is not for everyone; it requires the reader to make a giant leap of faith and accept some very powerful, if unusual concepts. However, for those unique individuals who are really ready to receive the message, 'The Secret Law of Attraction' is a life-changing discovery.

Rhonda Byrne's 'The Secret' took the ancient wisdom of the Law of Attraction and exposed it to a mass market but the real truth behind the activation of this law has nothing to do with positive thinking, mantras or acting like a 'rich person' to become rich.

Many people give up on the law of attraction before they discover the key to activating the true power of this divine function of the universe.

In this profound book, extended and updated for this third edition. New thought author Craig Beck shows you how to dramatically improve every aspect of your life by flowing with the divine energy already residing inside you.

- End your scarcity mindset
- Flood your life with abundance
- Experience happiness, peace and purpose
- Improve your health and heal those you love
- Awaken to the awesome power of divinity within you
- And much more

Chapter One

So, what brought you to this book? Is life is missing a few important things, maybe even something you can't quite put your finger on?

Most people discover the law of attraction because they believe there is something wrong or something missing in their lives. Whether you need more money, love, recognition or any other common human desire, it can all be summed up with one statement… 'You want to feel more happiness'. The things you desire are just egoic delivery mechanisms for happiness.

'I just want to be happy', a simple goal expressed as though it were the very least we could expect of life. Sadly, the vast majority of people live their lives in states ranging somewhere between mild discontentment to downright suicidal. Some are better at hiding it than others, but so many believe that true happiness is beyond their reach unless someone gives it to them.

More often than not the blame for this perpetual misery is laid at the door of the current financial predicament, and when asked how much of a pay rise would be needed to ensure a stress free, comfortable life, it's common for the answer to be double what their current salary is. They confidently declare that if they could only reach that new aspirational figure they would be happy for the rest of their lives. The reality is, if you granted their wish and repeated the exercise, no more than a year later they still wouldn't be happy with what they had. In the cold light of day this may appear to be just evidence of greed, but labeling it as such is pointless and simply goes to demonstrate the popular human propensity to lay blame.

Happiness is indeed a simple request, but most assume it is hidden and only the very few are fortunate enough to discover the treasure map that leads to its secret location. 'The Secret Law of Subconscious Attraction' will show you that you that not only do you already own the map, but you are currently standing right on top of the big red X that marks the spot of that buried treasure you crave so much. You will discover that you are born into this world with the potential to generate and experience joy beyond your wildest dreams. The power is within you; it has always been and can never be destroyed. The jigsaw is already complete, there are no missing pieces preventing it from working and it requires no external thing to make it complete.

The law of attraction is becoming increasingly exposed to a broader and wider commercial audience. Books such as Rhonda Byrne's 'The Secret' have brought what was once a niche concept to a mass market. As a result, many thousands of people around the world have completely changed their lives for the better. However, just as many have done what they thought they were being instructed to do and nothing has happen, some might even state that things have got considerably worse.

So why does the Law of Attraction work for some people and not for others? Simply put, there is another secret to 'The Secret'. By consciously applying this amazing and automatic law you are only meeting the universe half way. By dreaming of a new car or an unexpected promotion at work, and then consciously imagining yourself in that situation, doing all this is like filling the car with gas, starting the engine but not putting the gear shift into drive. Essentially you are left sitting on the driveway wondering why the car isn't moving!

You will discover as we make this journey together that the Law of Attraction ignores your conscious thoughts. The universe knows that you are quite capable of coming up with 100% proof nonsense as a result of listening to your ego, and thankfully protects you from manifesting some pretty appalling and disastrous things by deliberately discounting everything you think but don't believe. Only when a thought becomes a belief does the law actually kick in. When that dream of yours actually creates a bridge and sits not just in your awareness but also in your unconscious thoughts, only then does the magic start to flow.

Only the dreams of your subconscious can be manifest by the divine power within you, and without a bridge to carry the desire of your thinking mind over to this part of you, then your wishes will stay as exactly that forever more. If you prefer, think of this bridge as an electrical switch that when open and prevent the energy from flowing. All the power to create everything you ever dreamed of is within you, but this open switch is preventing the connection to the universe. If only you could find a way to reach inside your mind and close this switch, and in doing so allow your energy to flow into the universe, then magic would instantly and automatically appear in your life.

This book is an instruction manual that could just as easily be called 'how to close the switch', but I am not sure how many people would buy a book with a title like that. Certainly, if you find light switches complicated enough to require a how to guide you are probably not going to enjoy the rest of what I have to say!

Let me give a very common example of how most people fail to close the switch on a dream. Probably somewhere close to 75% of the western population is not happy with their body. Some are significantly obese and dream of the day they will be able to shop for clothes as freely as their slim friends. Others appear to be in perfect proportion but their own low self-esteem forces them to be over critical.

I spent many years as a photographer and nothing surprised me more than sitting down with a beautiful newly married woman to show her the wedding photographs to listen to her pick fault with herself over the smallest and sometimes even invisible things.

I approach photography as an art form, and so I was never the sort to accept just any wedding. I only wanted to shoot the most lavish and exotic of weddings where the photography was considered an exquisite and essential part of the day and not just something the couple feel obliged to have as part of their wedding package.

If you visit my photography website at www.CraigBeck.com you will see that I only work on a hand picked selection of weddings per year, and as such I am far from the cheapest option. I am only telling you this so I can rather bluntly get to the point that only beautiful people are willing to pay over the odds to get the photographer they want. It's a harsh reality of life that people who are not particularly attractive don't value photographs of themselves as much as the pretty people. Oh what a shallow world we live in, but as far as photography goes it's the elephant in the room that we really should admit to as a profession. We prefer to photograph the good-looking ones; there, I have said it!

I have taken stunning photographs of quite literally earth shatteringly beautiful brides and sat in bemusement as they stare at themselves in the photograph missing all the beauty to see something that isn't even there. They frown and wonder if their hair looks out of place or if their arm is too chubby.

We manifest what we believe and not what we think. Millions of people around the world who are overweight and dream daily of the thin self they would like to be. The only thing stopping the dream from becoming a reality and preventing them losing weight is the switch is stuck in the off position. They know that they want to be slim but they subconsciously believe the opposite to be the case. They unconsciously believe that they are fat and deserve to be just so. The switch is open and all the positive energy is blocked from flowing and thus, the universe delivers unto them exactly the image they created.

Flick the switch and all those images of the slim you flood into the subconscious and in that very same split second the universe responds in the blink of an eye to deliver what you now desire at a multi-conscious level.

So 'where is the switch' you may be screaming at the book. Patience is important at this point, because despite our western conditioning to believe we can own everything and anything we want. The switch is not something you can buy; it can't be owned. You don't need to be of a certain intellect or social strata to access it. The switch is nowhere physical, I can't point it out for you and there is no available map to locate it. It is not out there to be discovered, it is within, and you already hold it in your hand, but for the moment you choose not to be aware of it, never mind flick it closed.

It's not so ridiculous that we would assume that what we desire the most is to be found externally, virtually everything else we need certainly is. Food, air, water, heat and shelter are all external elements and logically we assume this theory applies to everything else in life that's worth having. The need for external components and attachments such as money, material possessions and even love are all demands of a part of the human mind called the ego.

When most people talk of the ego they are normally referring only to behavioral traits revolving around the traditional definition of the word. Ego is mostly considered to be a temporary expression of over-inflated self-confidence, demonstrated as conceit, selfishness and self-importance.

The ego is so much more that that narrow band of negative patterns, and yet that doesn't mean there is a good side to it, no aspect of the ego can be viewed in any sort of positive light or considered an advantage to the human existence. The ego is the little part of our physiological make-up that is quite frankly insane. Nobody is free of it, not even the most enlightened being. We all have differing strengths of ego and ergo according levels of insanity that present themselves in a myriad of different ways that we might label as character traits or personality.

The first thing you should know of this part of you, is that the ego cannot ever be satisfied, it can only ever be sedated temporarily. Like a naughty child at the 'all you can eat' ice cream factory, it will always want more no matter how much it gets, even if more of what you crave is in the long run detrimental to your well-being. It is for this reason alone that giving a person the exact amount of money they have declared will bring peace is only effective as a temporary sticking plaster solution to the problems. Very soon reasons why that amount was too conservative begin to emerge.

Unhappiness, pain and misery are human emotions created directly by the ego to manipulate a desired response. These painful feelings are generated by the 'thinking mind' when it doesn't get what it wants, but also rather ironically also directly as the result of giving it exactly what it wants too, such is the insanity!

Your ego can achieve peace only for the tiniest fragment of time, normally immediately after you give it what it wants. For the briefest of moments it affords you a small break from the insanity and stops relentlessly punishing and manipulating you. When the sedation begins to fade, the ego reawakens as ravenous as a grizzly bear stirring from a long hibernation. It demands more of what you gave it before, but ten times stronger, and will not accept anything but your capitulation, sending massive pain in the form of a hundred different negative emotions such as jealousy, low self-esteem and self loathing until it gets what it desires. This is the exact reason why 95% of diets fail; trying to arm wrestle the egoic mind into submission with a technique incorrectly labeled as 'will-power' is like trying to move a mountain with a spoon.

Nobody has ever achieved anything with 'will-power' because it's an oxymoron; there is actually no power involved in it at all! The ego cannot be strong-armed into submission by defiance; it has you outgunned on every level. Your ego has the power to cause you pain beyond your wildest nightmares, and it isn't afraid to use it. The only way you achieve anything of significance in life and

13

beat the discontentment of the ego is by harnessing the divine power of the subconscious. At this level of being you are capable of limitless joy, anything and everything is possible without the need for anything to make it possible. From contentment to perfection and everything in between, your subconscious mind has the power to deliver it to you.

What you believe about yourself in this state dictates what appears in your life. If at an unconscious level you no longer believe you are a smoker, then you will stop smoking, nothing your ego throws at you will either hurt or make the slightest impact on your journey to your goal, its delivery is as certain as night follows day.

Until this point I have carefully used the word subconscious, when really I would have preferred to say soul. I do this deliberately because for me to expect you to accept the word soul (and all its connotations) I have to make an assumption that you believe it exists in the first place. Virtually everyone accepts the concept of a conscious and a subconscious, I can comfortably bring these aspects of the human mind up nice and early in the book, but I wait until this point hoping to have whet your appetite before I appear to go 'all spiritual' on you!

For me your soul and your subconscious are one and the same because what happens to you unconsciously, and by that I mean without the interference of your ego or your thinking mind, happens with divine power. By divine I mean there is simply nothing that is impossible if your soul or subconscious so desires it. Naturally, the first skeptical objection to this grand claim of miracles is challenging statements like 'if I am all powerful, why aren't I rich already?' and so on.

The deeper answer to that question you will discover as you journey through this book, but as a temping morsel to keep you going; and of course to avoid 'question dodging' accusations flaring up so early in our relationship as author and reader, I would ask you to consider that it is only your ego that believes you need money to be happy. Anything that has its solution in the future is pure speculation of your conscious mind, one of those specific requirements of how happiness should be packaged for your consumption. Your soul doesn't believe anything; it desires nothing, needs nothing and it automatically knows what will make you happy.

As a natural born cynic myself, I will try and answer your logical objections as we discover these secrets together. By this point I understand that your mind is probably acting like the Hydra beast of Greek mythology; for every question I answer, two new ones appear to take its place. This is the ego again attempting to reassert its authority and we have been taught from an early age to listen to it.

From childhood we are told that to want too much is to be greedy, rich people are immoral and somehow tainted by their own success. Conversely, to not have enough money, to be poor, is also judged to be a failure. We project this confusing concept out to the masses through our movies, books, television, news and tabloid newspapers. We love the underdog until they become

15

successful and then we demand that they are brought down a peg or two.

Society wants us to have 'just enough' but not quite enough to be happy – this is what we have collectively agreed is 'normal' which for some reason when you write it down appears to be quite insanely ridiculous. Our parents also subscribed to this standpoint, as did their parents and all who went before them. It's the bizarre relay race of the ego forever passing its delusions onto the next generation. This is demonstrated by our parents in the vocalized desire for us to work hard and get a 'good job' to ensure our future happiness. What parents mean by a 'good job' is a safe and secure job that may even be boring but is continuous. Rarely do parents hope and dream that their children will follow their heart, throw caution to the wind and take risky, dangerous but exciting jobs.

There are many millions of people around the world in the most menial and insignificant of low paid, unskilled jobs that are content with their lot and truly happy within themselves, but no parent would wish or encourage this lifestyle for their child. Instead, their aspirations for their young are generated from the ego and they dream that they will be the world's next doctors, scientists, accountants, managers and directors. Hopefully, along the way they will meet the man or woman of their dreams, settling down with a mortgage (a word derived from the Latin phrase meaning until death) have kids and live happily ever after, only to repeat the process again.

16

A list of handed down expectations that compound the belief that happiness is a destination achievable through the attainment or attachment to external things. They want this for us because it's what they want for themselves and therefore assume it is also the best that could happen to us. This belief is an oasis in the desert to the thirsty man, nothing but a pure illusion.

This cycle has been running in the western world for many thousands of years, but recently levels of general unhappiness and frustration have begun to accelerate and magnify exponentially as a result of the stabilizing prop of traditional religion beginning to fail simultaneously. The discontented folk could previously be dissuaded from challenging the status quo with assurances that God has a place in heaven reserved for them, but only if they comply with the rules and dare not question the scriptures further.

As evidence for evolution grows more undeniable by the day, world leaders of mass religions continue to lose credibility by desperately clinging to an improbable and unlikely theory of creationism that is said to have happened just six thousand years ago. No longer are the masses kept in check by promises of an eternal reward in the afterlife as a justification for tolerating a life of discontentment here on earth.

Between 1998 and 2008 a million people stopped going to church on a Sunday. More recently, the much publicized abuse scandals within the Roman Catholic

Church have forced even the most devout follows to ask some serious questions of their own faith.

In the twenty-first century, increasing numbers of people are becoming less and less willing to blindly accept the word of traditional religion as an unquestionable truth. Despite the dramatic increase in shared agnosticism, the appetite for answers to the long-standing questions of mankind remain as strong as ever. This book is not about laying the blame of unhappiness at the door of religion; in some chapters you may even feel the reverse is being presented. Whilst I openly point the finger of ridicule at the unlikely and fantastical stories of the Old Testament, you will discover I have no allegiances and I am equally as likely to highlight the failings of the counter claims made by famous atheists and scientists alike.

By questioning everything that we have ever been told and combining the resulting fresh perception of what motivates and drives us as people with the knowledge of how our subconscious and thinking mind operates to deliver our dreams and of course nightmares, you will discover something quite breathtakingly amazing.

The Secret Law of Subconscious Attraction could be said to be just as much a book about avoiding unhappiness as it is about finding the opposite. Due to the unique configuration of our internal computer we call the mind, it is not possible to achieve a prospective of 'happiness' without the context of misery to give it meaning. In the same way you can't not think about an elephant unless you first think about an elephant.

In order to achieve happiness we have to consider the reverse of that emotion, as a result of this premise of human programming you will find that this book is not an instruction manual or a journey of discovery. If anything it's about the opposite of learning, an unlearning experience where we slowly strip away the false beliefs that you have been programmed and burdened with since birth.

When a fishing trawler gets trapped in a violent storm, what brings the respite is the removal of things and the arrival of nothing. The removal of the storm and a return to zero is what dissipates the sensation of peril and danger. As such, happiness is peace and peace is the absence of everything else, and so it's illogical to assume we can find what we are looking for by creating rules or by attaining material possessions.

The secrets revealed in this book will change your life forever, and your discovery of it at this point in your life is no coincidence. As the famous quotation goes; 'when the student is ready, the teacher will arrive', and for that reason, despite your excitement you cannot force this information onto others who do not seek it, do not expect them to receive the message with the same sense of wonder and excitement that you did.

Most people spend their entire lives trapped within the illusions of the egoic mind. However, a small and rapidly increasing number of people are awakening during their lifetime to realize the futility of their beliefs about what they think they 'need' to discover true peace and happiness on earth. You are one of the enlightened few that are ready to discover that the universe always ignores the dreams of your ego. However, using the core principles described in this book you will soon be able to manifest your dreams quickly and easily using the power of your subconscious.

Chapter Two
The Secret of 'The Secret'

By the spring of 2007, Rhonda Byrne had sold over four million copies her 'The Secret' book, and nearly two million DVD's of the movie. Now... Rhonda didn't invent the concept of the 'Law of Attraction' she was merely 'given' the inspiration to take the message to a new audience. Before Rhonda, modern day guru's such as Wayne Dyer, Joe Vitale and Jerry & Esther Hicks have been preaching the power of this invisible connection to 'the universe', or 'God' if you prefer, for many years.

'The Secret', and more recently the sequel 'The Power', is really just an account of how Rhonda discovered this amazing principle. It was studying these modern day interpretations of the power of the universe that I was able to step back from the confusing texts of traditional religion and discover several common themes that run through the core of every religious verse ever scribed. 'The Secret' by Rhonda exposes us to the universal law of attraction and suggests ways it can be used to get everything in life you desire. However, you can find evidence of a similar concept in the oldest of theories. Probably the most ancient of documented wisdom belongs to that of the Tao Te Ching (Dow De Jing) and the writings of an old Chinese master called Lao Tzu.

The Tau is the backbone on which most Chinese and other eastern spiritual beliefs are based, and it was originally written 500 years before the birth of Christ. So profound is it's wisdom that it has been translated many hundreds of times and its teachings are spread across the world, often without students being aware of the source of its message. One of the most famous phrases that I am sure you have heard is 'the journey of a thousand miles starts with one step'.

Essentially the Tao Te Ching tells us not only to be aware of that inner force; call it God, source or the universe if you prefer (the name you give it is not relevant), but to also give in trying to control it and in doing so stop trying to control the direction of your life. Rather, see your life on earth like a river, a flowing stream of water. You came from a source exactly the same way a river begins it's journey... from the ocean, it transmutes to a gas and joins the clouds before reforming as a rain drop and so begins the process over again. The river takes the path of least resistance to get back to its source. It never struggles to change direction or to go in an unnatural path, it takes every inch forward as its only concern. Where it has been and the path to come is irrelevant.

Slowly but surely as I read more and more theories from ancient eastern philosophies to the Hawaiian healing systems of Ho'oponopono, I began to feel alive again. I can only describe the sensation as throwing kindling onto a fire that had all but extinguished itself and sitting back to watch it roar back into life. I could clearly see that there were common traits that ran through the heart of all the major religions and belief systems, but all had been translated and expressed in different ways. In our ego driven desire to be the holder or owner of the truth, each religion in turn decried that it was the only true word of God. As the ego demanded, wars were declared to force the point home.

If you want to read more about my own personal journey from atheism to a logical spiritual conclusion, read my book 'The God Enigma' available from www.craigbeckmedia.com.

Here and now I am going to tell you the eight secrets I discovered to creating true peace, happiness and abundance in your life. However, I warn you that you must be prepared to take a leap of faith. There may a statement that you read here that you disagree with or don't understand. All I ask is, while you are using one of the many Subconscious programming audio books from SubAttraction.com, you trust me and live by these principles. The biggest problem for discoverers of the Law of Attraction through books such as 'The Secret' is they try what they have been told and it doesn't appear to work. The reason there are so many individuals around who are ready to tell you that they tried 'The Secret' and it failed, is because they were only 'consciously' asking for things to be delivered in their life. The conscious mind is human; it is weak and constitutes only about 10% of your brain activity. Trying to consciously create abundance in your life is akin to moving a mountain with a spoon.

In my book 'The God Enigma' I fully explain why and answer many of the questions that are already popping into your curious mind. Here and now I am assuming you are about to listen to one of my Subconscious Attraction downloads and I want to get you into the correct frame of mind to get maximum results. I don't know what your goal is, it could be attracting more money, getting out of debt, quitting smoking, winning the lottery or finding your soul mate. You will find all the systems you need to deal with all aspects of you life (or ego) at subattraction.com.

Here are the eight principles you need to know before you listen to an audio download:

Chapter Three
Principle One – Let go and let God

This is the most important principle of The Secret Law of Subconscious Attraction, so pay particular attention to the next chapter.

Let go and let God! Accept that your conscious thoughts are largely irrelevant and stop trying to control life, yours or anyone else's. The biggest acceptance you can make on the journey to true success and abundance is that of acknowledging that divinity or the universe has a plan for you. Do you not think God already knows everything you want before you ask for it? So stop asking; the universe knows what your ego wants and it also knows what is best for you. Give up trying to control the uncontrollable and your life will instantly change for the better.

The recurring message of this book is to highlight the continuous futility of searching the external world for happiness when embedded with you is everything you need, want and dream of. Of course, only the rare few discover that the pot of gold is never at the end of the rainbow but actually hidden within its majestic beauty. So again you might question, if this power resides within, why it doesn't seize control of our lives and stop us making those bad choices and mistakes, why does it allow the ego to play this futile game?

Free will is all too often offered as an explanation to the unexplainable. But with a little thought you can see that without free will, life is actually pointless. Without mistakes we can't learn, discover or evolve. Take away free will and not only do you lose the opportunity to experience the bad emotions and feelings of life, but as there can be no ying without yang it would also prevent the experience of all the joy and positive outcomes possible on earth too.

Hidden in the depths of the most traumatic periods of your life are the most profound and powerful messages waiting to be discovered, or remembered if you prefer. This doesn't mean you need to be a slave to your ego, you have the choice to observe it where once you would blindly act on its orders. As you begin to detach from its grip over you, its voice gets weaker, its power fades. What is left behind is silence and in that peace you will begin to feel your soul communicating with you and reminding you who you really are.

In the egoic trap of modern day life we just don't allow the subconscious the silence it needs to hear what the soul desires as it is too busy running the erroneous programmes we have developed over the years. Each one of these dysfunctional routines has been hand crafted by the ego, yours or the collective ego of society. Thoughts derived from fear that are then repeated and amplified so many times they become physical and embed themselves in the unconscious mind for automatic completion. By physical I don't just mean they cause real events and things to appear in your life, they actually create new tissue and cells within your brain.

Research on primates has shown than if you restrict the movement of one part of a monkeys body (e.g. his left arm), over time the cells in its brain dedicated for use by the opposing limb multiply and grow. This is why negative habits are so hard to overcome, you are not just battling an embedded belief but you have to deconstruct physical pathways in the brain.

The biggest fear of your ego is the sensation of loss, driven ultimately from the biggest loss of all, death. If you force your conscious mind to experience any form of loss it will hit back with massive levels of emotional pain until you return or replace what it was attached to. This is evident in its strongest form when we suffer bereavement. I am sure you will know first hand just how much pain is involved in grief. This pain is generated by an ego which has been doubly wounded, first by the removal of love, attention and affection from the person who has died and can no longer service those specific needs, but also because it reminds your ego of its own ultimate fate. You also experience lesser but still very painful forms of this egoic reaction when someone steals from you, a relationship ends or you lose your job. All forms loss cause major trauma to your conscious mind, and it doesn't take it at all well, kicking and screaming like a tempestuous child until it is pacified. In the same way you wouldn't give a child everything it demands, your approach toward the ego should be the same.

Knowledge is power and understanding that loss is the big red panic button for your conscious mind that allows you to step back from the pain and observe it rather than experience it. The sensation of loss is so feared by the ego because it plays on our earliest and most basic of fears. We come into the world completely dependent on others, without the love and care of our parents we would quickly perish a die. For the first few years of our life our mother and father are essentially Gods in our eyes. Giant, imposing beings with the power to apparently fix all problems, make any uncomfortable circumstance feel right again and with seemingly the most insignificant of gestures, often nothing more than a hug will suffice. To a certain extent this belief can stay with us throughout our developing years through to our late teens and early adult life.

My grandfather Jack was a steel worker by profession; biceps like tree trunks, standing well over six foot tall, he was through my young eyes nothing less than an invincible giant. As a young boy he would sometimes take me to the steel foundry where he worked, I would watch in awe as he manhandled giant steel girders into the pressing machine he operated.

One day as I watched him working, a piece of hot steel sheered off the machine and shot like a bullet towards my grandfather. The searing metal ripped through the skin of his muscled bicep causing a shallow but long cut to seep blood through the fabric of his overall. I winced and grimaced as I almost experience the intense pain for myself, such was the shock that hit me in that moment.

As tears welled up in my eyes as I looked at the blood running down my grandfather's arm. I had expectations of how he should react to that amount of pain, how any mortal would respond to such an injury, but I was amazed by his reaction, he glanced down at the wound and shook his head as though annoyed at the inconvenience of it and simply carried on with his work.

He finished the girder he was working on before calmly walking off to the first aid box where he wiped down the cut and gave me a reassuring smile. That day he effectively became a man of super hero status to me, and not until I was 13 years old did I see any evidence of fallibility in this man I adored. Jack was married to Lilly, my grandmother who had been a heavy smoker for as long as I had been around. In the late eighties at the young age of 63, her lungs finally decided they could take no more abuse, gave up the fight and she passed away in Darlington Memorial hospital in the North East of England.

At the funeral I sat and watched my grandfather sitting alone on the church pew, his eyes staring forward at the coffin but not really looking at it, lost in a thousand thoughts, regrets and missed opportunities. Slowly a single tear rolled down his cheek and he dabbed it away with his handkerchief. This simple and natural reaction hit me like a ton of bricks, I had never seen this man beaten by anything, he was invincible, and to see that belief proved incorrect was almost as upsetting as the funeral itself.

By the time we can talk we are so addicted to love and attention we will literally do anything to get it. If you are a parent you will be aware of how badly children can misbehave as a route to getting any form of attention. The ego has developed and become so hooked it would rather take the easy route and have negative attention than nothing at all. As long suffering parents we inadvertently use and manipulate this egoic fear of loss in our children to solicit good behavior. Most punishments handed out to youngsters involve some form of loss… the removal of toys, not being allowed to play with friends, banned from watching TV, and most scary of all, the perceived removal of love.

Whilst these punishments achieve a short term goal of compliance, it compounds the conditioning of the child to be forever a slave to the pain generated by the ego. The perception of removal of love is the most terrifying thing imaginable to a young mind, and when parents inadvertently stumble across the effectiveness of this punishment they incorrectly observe its power and use it repeatedly to swiftly ensure compliance in a wide range of scenarios. All these punishments are direct attacks on the ego, but exactly like a naughty child, the 'thinking mind' doesn't care what sort of attention it gets as long as it gets some form of identification, a confirmation of significance.

The way we discipline and control our children will often set in motion one of the major cycles of unhappiness that run throughout our life… the need to comply with the demands, wishes and rules of others in order to attract positive attention.

True happiness is never dependent upon the actions or approval of others, and joy in all its forms comes essentially from an awareness of that freedom. You simply cannot be free while you still believe the input from other humans is in anyway necessary. Our parents, teachers, politicians and traditional religion all tell us repeatedly that to conform to their rules is good and anything else is evil. As you will discover later in this book your first instinct is more significant than you ever might have assumed. This instinctive response to any significant situation is what I call 'The Primary Thought Event', I will explain the power of this shortly.

Obedience and conformity are not natural, and for the spiritually minded nor are they a requirement of God. Does anyone instinctively feel good about paying taxes, doing their homework or depriving oneself of pleasure in order to satisfy what we are led to believe is a desire of our God?

Over the last generation thousands of new rules have been thought up by politicians who believed they could sit atop an ivory tower and dictate how for societies own good it should comply with their rules. Whilst at the same time the very same politicians fiddled their expenses and grew rich on the proceeds. All rules are man made and what lies at the heart of every one of them is the premise that in order for someone to be happy, someone else must behave in a specific way. Put simply, its more evidence of mans continued search for contentment where it does not reside, externally.

Think about it logically; over the past few centuries, as western society has become more and more 'civilized', we have invented literally thousands of new rules, each with the goal of making life better. We have quite rightly declared that everything from murder to speeding is wrong and must be severely punished, but have we actually managed to eradicate these negative behaviors by pronouncing more rules surrounding them? No, and in most cases we caused a dramatic increase in their occurrence in popular culture. If inventing rules really worked there would be no more war, sexual assault would be a thing of the past and you could once again leave your front door unlocked whilst you went shopping as our relatives tell us they used to be able to do.

Every year in the UK in the month of March the government declares a day to be 'no smoking day', a prescribed date when the state health department wants the nations smokers to quit, at least for 24 hours, or even better still, forever. What do you think happens to the consumption of cigarettes on 'no smoking day'? That's right, it goes up! Why? Simply because human beings instinctively don't like being told what to do. Despite knowing deep down inside that the effects of nicotine and inhaling toxic smoke is causing them significant and lasting harm, smokers smoke more purely as an act of defiance to the rules. The ego does not like losing control whether that is to your subconscious or to the requirements of other people.

This chapter of 'The Secret Law of Subconscious Attraction' may appear at first glance to be inciting mass anarchy. It's true that a complete abandonment of the rules of society would cause chaos and possibly even destruction of the human race. Only enlightened souls can function effectively and successfully co-exist in this utopian environment, because they understand the fruitlessness of destructive acts against others, and that the only place you can find a path to love, peace and happiness comes from within.

Awakened souls know that there is really no need for rules because inside we have our own divine navigation system ready to show us the correct path. We all have this in-built GPS system, but most simply choose not to use it, which is similar to setting off on a long journey without considering where you are going. Our soul is constantly trying to tell us the route we need to take and that communication comes in the form of something called a 'Primary Thought Event'. These are powerful messages that you get everyday of your life but for the most part ignore or allow your ego to counter argue before you get chance to act. Later I will explain in detail how you hear this divine direction, and more importantly how you act on it before your conscious has time to talk you out of it.

Without explaining it further than that, I can still easily demonstrate the existence of this internal moral guidance system, and prove that you don't need laws and rules at the same time. If I told you to walk into a shop and steal some food, how would you feel about yourself as you sat eating your stolen lunch? Would you feel bad about yourself because of the rules or because something inside you makes you feel that what you have just done doesn't serve you. This act of theft can't possibly serve you, as in order to accomplish it, you first have to hurt someone else. As we have already agreed, everything on earth is as one. All things, people and animals are all constructed from the same big ball of modeling clay and it is not possible to hurt someone else without hurting yourself.

On earth at the moment there are seven billion human souls all at different levels of enlightenment. Many have just begun their journey and remember virtually nothing of who they really are, whilst others are so awake that they want for nothing, need nothing and desire nothing other than the opportunity to help others. Your discovery of this book is no coincidence or mistake, for if it were you would have surely stopped reading by this point. Similar to a smart bomb, the secrets in this book seek out and attract like-minded people to its knowledge. As you slowly remember who you really are, often over many lifetimes you gently and cautiously allow the eternal part of you to take more and more control over your decisions and direction in life.

If you try to explain, or worse still preach, the contents of this book to others who are less advanced on their journey of awakening, you will be met with at best ridicule and in the worst cases anger, resentment and personal insults. People who are not ready for this message are not to be considered inferior, for such an attitude is best left to traditional religion.

For me, walking into an unfamiliar church always feels similar to the scenes from old westerns where a stranger walks into a bar and abruptly the music and chatter stops as the congregation turn to suspiciously weigh up the newcomer. There is a thick air of smugness and pomposity from the regular attendees who know all the lyrics to all the hymns and will sing as loud as they can to demonstrate how dedicated to their cause they are. This is purely an act of the ego disguised as superiority.

The collective attitude of many church congregations is breathtaking in its hypocrisy. Imagine for a moment that I walk into a traditional church service on any given Sunday morning and take my place in the front pew. I am dressed in ripped jeans, sleeveless vest which shows off my heavily tattooed arms and chest. My hair is spiked, dyed and my nose and ears are pierced with studs. Do you believe the church regulars would be happy to see another person joining their gang to share in the love of their God, or do you think it more likely that they would tut and shake their head at me? Religion's that preach of the threats of an angry deity actually encourage their members to question, judge and declare fault with others. In short, they direct their follows to act like the ego, which is the polar opposite of the soul.

Do not feel the need to preach this message to others, they will reach the point in their own personal journey when they are ready for this information in their own good

35

time. There is no rush, actually there is a whole eternity in which to complete the task and even then when you can see the true reality of life for what it is, at the point where you have remembered how perfect you are and there is nothing more to experience beyond perfection itself, you can decide to forget it all and begin the journey over again in an infinite loop of remembering.

A common objection (from one unprepared for this message) to my statements of our divine aversion to anything resembling a rule or law, will be an angrily phrased question such as 'surely without laws someone could just come into my house and steal anything he wanted?' Maybe you are wondering for yourself just how society would work in this environment and maybe you are right to question it. Maybe it wouldn't work at all, but it's all irrelevant because these questions fail to appreciate that your attachment to all physical things is just more evidence of your conscious mind at work. As Jesus said 'If someone takes your coat, let him have your shirt as well'. Even attachment to other people is purely driven by your ego.

In the extreme case of murder, the person you care about returns to a state of pure love, pure perfection, and the soul is once more free from the constraints and limitations of the human body. The pain is all yours, not theirs, and is created by that deep-seated fear of loss.

In a perfect world where mankind had somehow managed to shake off the curse of the thinking mind and followed the desire of the subconscious, there would be no crime as nobody would see other people's possessions as a threat to their own sense of self. There would be no murder as jealousy, resentment, hate and all other negative emotions would no longer be possible. To experience this utopian dream on earth, society would have to awaken on mass at the same time. Of course, this will never happen and is the same reason why man will continue to seek happiness at the expense of others until eventually we do so much damage the planet becomes incapable of sustaining life.

Does that mean you should accept defeat and carry on being a slave to your ego and accept living with a 'if you can't beat them, join them' mentality? Of course not, that view again propagates the illusion that your happiness is dependent upon other people complying with your wishes, and by now I am hoping you are starting to see the opposite is very much the case.

I am blessed with two wonderful and amazing children, a little girl called Aoife who is 10 and I can't believe Jordan, the little boy I used to bounce on my knee is now a 14 year old six foot tall rugby player with a six pack and defined muscles I never had even in the prime of my youth. They are both perfectly healthy and happy with excellent eyesight and hearing, but surprisingly when I shout upstairs and tell them to turn off the television and get some sleep their hearing is worryingly poor, in fact, I would describe them as being completely and profoundly deaf children. I am pretty sure it's nothing to do with the acoustics of our home because when I whisper to my wife that we should maybe order in pizza for the night, they are downstairs and salivating like Pavlov's dogs before I have finished the sentence.

We are all extremely talented and diligent information cherry pickers. Within us is a clear path to happiness, but we simply choose not to listen. A good physical world analogy would be to carry around the winning lottery numbers in your handbag but decide never to play them, and then after the draw get annoyed and upset because you are still not as wealthy as you want to be.

The ego makes predictions of the future based on events of the past; it speculates that what has gone before is likely to happen again. If you were brought up in a family that believed that money was hard to come by and that wealth was the trappings of the rich (other people) and not the everyday man, then your ego will predict that there will be more of the same in the future. Life becomes one big self-fulfilling prophecy, is it not true that overweight parents often bring up overweight children who go on to struggle with their weight for the rest of their lives?

The ego creates judgments and opinions on everything in your life, from how you feel about specific people to what food you like and every other aspect of daily life. Because everything created by the ego will have been born out of the raw emotion of fear, it will have significant aspects to it that are incorrect.

For example, you may believe that your friend James is tight with money and never pays his fair share when you are socializing together. This is a subjective opinion of your ego based on your own attachment to and fear of losing material possessions. Your ego worries that if you are spending more than your fair share on other people, there might not be enough left for you; after all, money is hard to come by, right? You are making judgments without having access to the full facts. The reality of James' spending habits are unknown, he could be saving money to pay for his old mum's operation or he could indeed just have an ego equally pessimistic about money as you do. Who knows, or cares? The truth is irrelevant and makes no difference to the point I am making here.

This opinion of the ego is always a "Secondary Thought Event', in other words, whilst you come to these judgments in the blink of an eye, faster than any modern day computer, they still cross the finishing line into your mind in a clear second place. There is a thought that comes half a second before these opinions, and this is called 'The Primary Thought Event (PTE)'. A PTE only happens when you come across a situation that questions who you really are as a person.

Normally PTE's happen around questions of integrity and you are unlikely to feel its presence whilst trying to decide what flavor ice cream to buy at the cinema or which pair of shoes to wear on a night out at an expensive restaurant. However, in circumstances of merit, this voice is very audible, but despite that clarity, in most cases the first thing your ego does is argue that you should ignore it. Often a PTE will cause severe distress to your ego because it may suggest detachment from something material or it may show a blatant disregard for something your conscious mind identifies with, such as money or personal possessions.

Let me paint a picture for you, a typical example of the PTE being ignored… A city worker pushed open the thick glass door of his air-conditioned office and walked out into the warm muggy air of the busy street. His expensive suit cuts him a fine and respectable figure as he walks to the nearby deli to pick up a sandwich and orange juice for his lunch.

On route, no more than fifty meters from his office door, he spots a young man slumped on the floor begging for loose change. He must be no more than 19 years old, his clothes are dirty and torn and he has an expression of hopelessness etched into his young face. He is not bothering people, just simply holding out a scrawny, limp and defeated hand for any coins. BANG! A PTE happens that clearly says 'give then man money, give him lots of money', it says to the city gent 'you have plenty, and even if you emptied all the notes from your wallet it wouldn't make any difference you would just refill the wallet from the abundance that you have'. This opinion represents who you are at a divine level, it is the voice of your soul, or if you want, a more grandiose statement; this is the voice of God. Less than half a second later the ego goes into panic at the thought that he might actually be considering 'giving this person all our money'.

The ego, with a scarcity mindset, has alarm bells ringing all over the place and it begins to argue that it would be ridiculous to give all the money to this man, because then there wouldn't be enough left to buy lunch. As he gets closer to the homeless man his mind is in turmoil. He feels that he should give the man money but can't argue against the strong position of the conscious mind. The ego suggests a compromise; maybe just a few coins would be better and more appropriate than the folding stuff. Desperately the man hunts in his pocket for loose change. He can't find any and his ego advises to avoid looking bad he simply crosses the road to skip the situation altogether.

So the man crosses the road and continues his journey to the sandwich shop, the down and out who really needed the money got nothing and the gentleman who was talked out of responding to the PTE lost the opportunity to experience the joy of giving to another and flowing in the same direction as his soul.

Did the city worker do a bad thing? No, as we have previously stated, good and bad are always subjective, the homeless man may have used that money to clean himself up and eat a decent meal, or he could just have likely spent it on alcohol or hard drugs. No act is either good or bad but rather is a decision that either serves us or doesn't serve us.

When you follow the PTE you allow perfection to flow into your life, it's the gift that keeps giving. The person you helped benefits (although this is almost irrelevant), you also benefit by doing something that 'serves you' and your act of selecting to permit divinity to act in defiance of the ego causes disruption to the power of the conscious mind. Every time the ego is prevented from controlling your response to life's events, it gets a fraction of a percent weaker as a result.

Do this often enough and the effect on your ego is compounded, slowly you start trusting your thoughts less and start acting in flow with God more.

Chapter Four
Principle Two - Accept responsibility for everything in your life

Actually THIS is the most important principle of The Secret Law of Subconscious Attraction, so get your eagle eyes ready to learn this stuff.

Blame is nothing but the vocalization of a wounded ego. It achieves nothing, changes nothing and is a pointless act. The only good thing you can derive from the act of blaming is that it clearly identifies when the ego is manipulating you.

Many years ago a good friend of mine called Denise came to visit me. It was only a short journey down the motorway of around twenty miles, but when she finally reached my home she was shaking with fear, her face streaked with mascara that had ran like a river down her cheeks. She hugged me tightly when I opened the door and pushed her way into the house. It took me several minutes to calm her down and find out what had happened on that journey. This is the story she told me:

She had left her home at just before three in the afternoon, we had no specific plans and no appointments to meet so we hadn't bothered to arrange a time to get together; any time in the afternoon was just fine. She had planned to take a slow drive over and we were to grab a coffee at Starbucks and just have a good old catch up.

She had a cute little Fiat Panda that was affectionately referred to as Freddie the Fiat. As Denise pulled onto the motorway, her stereo blaring out her favorite tunes, a large supped-up BMW came speeding up to her rear bumper. Even though the driver had space to overtake he chose to intimidate her by getting as close to the rear of her car as possible.

At this point Denise became the second person in this story to respond to the demands of their ego. She pressed her foot to the floor and accelerated. Glancing into her rear view mirror she mouthed some choice insults at the guy behind. Acknowledging her defiance he kept pace before pulling alongside to further intimidate Denise.

Now my friend Denise may drive a very feminine car and have a cute nickname for it, but don't be under any illusion about her self-confidence. She is certainly no shrinking violet and promptly gave the aggressive driver the finger. This made his blood boil and whatever else he had planned for that afternoon soon became a secondary objective. Rather than accelerating away, which his car was more than capable of doing against the 1.2 liter engine of Denise's Fiat, he pulled back in behind her and matched her speed.

For twenty miles the BMW stayed no more than six foot from the trunk of her little red car. Denise was by now extremely paranoid and scared about who this was. She had come off the motorway to get away from him but the BMW followed and clung to her tail. She had tried slowing down to a virtual snails pace hoping he would get bored and overtake. Denise even pushed that Fiat to the limits of its inferior engine to try and escape this now very threatening person.

He followed her right up to the driveway to my home, only when I opened the door and let her push past me into the hallway did he rev the engine hard and, wheels spinning, accelerate away.

So here is the question, whose fault was that little drama?

Whether you think it's Denise's fault or the other driver is largely irrelevant. Blame is in itself irrelevant because it is only the opinion of the conscious ego. This whole unpleasant episode was just a physical materialization of two egos attempting to protect an internal perception of reality. The BMW driver believes at an egoic level that having a big and powerful car makes him equally as big and powerful. His ego tells him that if he then drives this beast of a machine in an aggressive and threatening manner, then he will become more important than other people on the road. This misguided person is so conditioned by the insane part of his mind that he now sees this behavior as a confirmation of his own significance.

When his threats are not accepted or even worse challenged by a headstrong individual like Denise, this is a double assault on his ego. Firstly, her refusal to be scared of him wounds his belief that he is a powerful person who people should be afraid of. Secondly, he is suffering from grief, the loss of something he thought he owned, and this is the most upsetting thing you can inflict on any ego.

The conscious thinking mind despises any form of loss because it uncomfortably reminds it that one day it will suffer the biggest loss of all. The only way to stop the pain is for the thinking mind to attempt to regain the perception of control. The ego believes that if it can retake the significant position then it will prove that it can achieve the impossible... permanency.

So at this point in the drama, the ego of the first driver is driving the BMW and Denise's own ego is about the take the wheel of the Fiat. Rather than shrug and smile as the offending vehicle approached, her ego saw this as an attempt to take significance from her. Panicked into action by her own potential loss, she retaliates to the aggressor with an act in kind.

Two egos are now locked into a battle for control of the situation and in a war to preserve identification with the self-generated images of who these individuals believe they are. Denise was lucky to escape with the scare that she got, but did she learn anything from the experience? As she sat and told me what an idiot that guy was and how if she ever saw him again she would be doing this and doing that, it became obvious that her ego had been badly wounded.

Blame is the reaction of a wounded ego that can't accept a loss. Denise could not accept at a conscious level that she wasn't the invincible, powerfully independent woman that she had become identified with. The fact that she needed to run to me for protection caused a deep egoic wound that would need to be explained away quickly.

You must accept responsibility for everything in your life, and I really do mean everything. This means you cannot blame anyone, anything or any circumstance for any problem in your life today. All things in your life were attracted or created by you. This is perhaps the most difficult aspect of subconscious attraction to accept. Many people I speak to initially object very strongly to this statement and respond with statements such as 'I hate being overweight, I was a big child and now I am a big adult, and you have the audacity to say it's all my fault' or even stronger than that, I have had 'half my phobias and anxiety today are as a direct result of being abused as a child, are you really suggesting I am responsible for what that man did to me'. With such powerful sentiment as that, I can understand how hard a concept it is to take on board, but whilst those events are certainly not their fault they most definitely are their responsibility.

We are the creators of our own universe and whether by divine intervention or by following our ego, we manifest everything we experience. Taking 100% responsibility for everything in our world is the first step on the path to letting go.

I never promised you this would be easy, and if this rule of subconscious attraction wasn't difficult enough to swallow I would like to make it even more challenging for you. You must also accept that other people's problems that you become aware of are now also your responsibility. Why? Because, you are the creator of your own universe and as such everything in your life is there because you subconsciously placed it there.

If you are approached by a work colleague who tells you he is very ill and the doctors say he needs urgent treatment or the future looks bleak. This situation was brought to you not by accident but by your subconscious connection to the divine, which in turn is connected to every other object on the earth. We struggle with this concept because unlike a tree we are not rooted to the planet, therefore we live under the illusion we are somehow separate and independent of it. The same 'Fragment Of God' that resides in you is identical to the fragment that lives in your colleague, to that of your enemy, to that of the stranger sat next to you on the bus, to the homeless man in the street! At your core you are the same raw material. Which, on a basic level shows you the fruitlessness of racism and on a deeper level demonstrates how feelings of superiority over someone or the reverse of that are both delusions of the ego. You are no more and no less than your brother because you are essentially the same entity separated temporarily by a physical body. When the river reaches the ocean all will become one again.

This rule is so important because now you understand that the blocks in your subconscious are not just effecting you but those around you, and it means you can begin clearing the bad programming that is causing your child to be bullied at school, your wife to be ill or your father to be addicted to gambling and so on.

To use the Secret Law of Subconscious Attraction effectively you absolutely must accept that everything is perfect just as it is. The universe is the very embodiment of pure perfection, nothing is a mistake and absolutely everything happens by design. Is it even a reasonable consideration that a perfect deity could ever make an error in his act of creation?

This means the child born with a terrible disability is perfect, the earthquake is perfect and you losing your job is perfect. Everything is there because you wanted it to be there, your ego will insist that you find some other person to blame for all these events, and if you can't find a human to accuse then it will apply a broadsword attack at God. When our collective egos fail to point the finger at someone on earth we point to the heavens and declare it 'an act of God'. But just wait a minute… Everything is an act of God; good, bad or indifferent.

It's tough to accept that a child born with a disability serves any purpose to God, but if it didn't it wouldn't happen. As you will discover later in this book, what makes it appear 'bad' to us is our preoccupation with time. If you can step back from who you believe you are, forget what you currently look like and ignore your conditioned beliefs and attachments and see life as just the theatrical production that it really is. Remember again that you are just an actor playing a part in the script and step outside the character to view yourself as the actor, the eternal being that you really are. Only with this bigger picture mindset can the negativity of all situations begin to fade away.

Let's imagine that in the case of this baby born with severe health problems, the soul that resides within its compromised human body has lived 600 previous lives spanning 33,000 years on earth. Over those thousands of years this soul has used the experience of physical existence on earth to move closer and closer to God, slowly lifetime by lifetime discovering more and more about the real truth of existence. Over those thousands of years and hundreds of lives this soul has experienced everything. It has been male, female, straight, gay, white, black, rich, poor, powerful and a down and out. If its experience of year 33,001 is spent in the form of a disabled child, do you believe this provides no useful purpose, nothing can be experienced that adds to all the previous able-bodied lifetimes?

Our ego insists that this is all there is, if it doesn't happen in this lifetime then it doesn't matter. It screams this at you 24/7 because, for it, that is very much the truth. At the end of this life your current ego will rot in a grave along with the rest of your earthly body. However, the real you will simply change form and carry on forever and ever into eternity.

If you can grasp the truth that you are eternal and all that really ends is your current character in the script of this great universal movie, then you can also appreciate from the point of view of God; pain and discomfort are mere blips in the beautiful and joyful process of remembering that is life. We choose to experience a physical life on earth because it gives us the opportunity to feel the wonderful emotions of the world; life is truly a priceless gift.

To give you a comparison that your ego will be able to appreciate, life is like me offering you a billion dollars but in order to get the cash I need you to experience the most intense and traumatic pain imaginable for 0.01 of a second. Would you take the cash?

Of course you would, and that is why we keep coming back to experience life on earth. We know there will be misery and pain but the overall positive experience massively outweighs the negatives when those experiences are allowed to appreciate across an infinite timeline. Some lives will be amazing, while others will be painful, but the collective experience is perfection.

Part of the process of becoming a master of the law of subconscious attraction is seeing the beauty and opportunity in everything and having the foresight to observe your pain for the message that it is without experiencing the dark despair the ego would have you believe is an unavoidable part of life. If there are things in your life currently causing you pain then you have the divine power to change them, all you have to do is flick the switch.

True happiness within this lifetime comes from the removal of internal conflict, not from the removal of external irritations. All unhappiness stems from the ego's refusal to accept and be grateful for the present moment. The pain you feel and describe as unhappiness or depression is the force being applied on you by the ego incorrectly assuming the future and past will be and was a better place to be. As soon as you stop swimming upstream, acknowledge the ego but ignore its demands and accept the moment and all it brings with it, then you will be free. The good news is happiness is the default byproduct of freedom.

To disable the ego in the lowest times where you would describe yourself as feeling very unhappy with life, you must find a way to no longer see a benefit in what you believe you need to be happy. Only once the benefit is removed can the power be reduced. This is the reason why virtually all smokers fail to quit without some sort of intervention or help. As long as they still believe the cigarettes are providing an enhancement to their life (be that stress reduction or weight control) they will never stop, because the only weapon in their arsenal is will power. You are about to discover that will power is a gun loaded with blanks, for all intents and purposes it looks, feels and acts like an effective weapon. Secretly it is completely ineffective.

Repetition is the mother of all learning and the human brain is so awe-inspiring that it actually responds to your most frequent activities and thoughts by creating new physical pathways to process the tasks that are important to you. This quite literally means that if I took a scan of your brain before strapping your preferred hand to your side for three months, thereby forcing you to use your weaker limb for everyday tasks. A second brain scan at a later date would reveal that your brain had physically changed. Some areas would be denser and more eclectically active than before, and other areas would appear to have shrunk in size.

One of the most effective ways to prevent degenerative mental illnesses such as dementia and Alzheimer's disease is to remain cognitively challenged as long as possible. Elderly people are advised to keep socializing, meet new people, read books and even do the daily crossword. The reason for this is when you stimulate the brain it grows and absorbs more energy, which keeps it healthy. If you allow it to vegetate, the brain becomes less significant and actually reduces in size and strength.

The upside of this amazing feature of the human mind is that there is potentially a limitless spectrum of information we can absorb. We can continue learning and experiencing for as long as we choose to and the brain will adapt and change to best serve us. The downside is this action has no filter; the brain will strengthen and get better at something whether it is beneficial or harmful to you. Normally when the brain creates a new neural pathway around a negative behavior we call it a habit or addiction.

When we identify one of these negative pathways and decide that we are going to change a behavior, we are often surprised at how difficult it is. My son Jordan is a nail biter, he always has been and simply can't stop. We have tried everything from coating his nails with a foul tasting deterrent to simply pointing out his habit every time he does it. One day as he sat chewing away I snapped at him 'Jordan, please stop chewing your nails'. He looked at me completely bemused and said 'I want to but I don't even know I am doing it, so how can I stop?'

And here is the rub; when your brain creates a physical piece of tissue to carry out a task, it becomes automatic, and by that I mean not requiring conscious thoughts to activate. There is physical hard wiring to beat your heart and make you breathe in and out. Thankfully we don't have to consciously decide to breath. In the case of my son there is a tiny fragment inside his head that makes him chew his nails. The only way to stop him chewing his nails is to take away this pathway. Shouting at him won't do a thing, anymore than telling an alcoholic that drinking is killing him or a smoker that the cigarettes will probably give her lung cancer, will affect their behavior.

Smokers know what they are doing is life threateningly bad, but still they can't stop lighting up and sucking away on their cancer sticks. When smokers do stop one of the most common complaints is that they feel uncomfortable not having anything to hold in their hand. Many begin carrying a pen around in their hand as a substitute for the missing appendage. The brain expects there to be a cigarette in the hand and it is so conditioned to this sensation that when it is removed it creates anxiety.

The definition of insanity is repeatedly doing something the same way and expecting the outcome to change. When people become unhappy with an area of their life and decide they want to change it, they virtually always turn to will-power as the solution. Overweight individuals force themselves to avoid the food they so desperately want to eat, smokers spend the day cranky and irritable daydreaming of the cigarette they desire but are painfully trying to resist.

You have probably heard the much touted statistic that 95% of people who go on a diet, within two years have not only put the weight back on, but added an additional five pounds of fat. Alcoholics Anonymous has a success rate just over 5%, meaning slightly under 95% of their members will seriously relapse.

Will-Power is an oxymoron; it's like pushing a revolving door hard and wondering why you keep getting hit on the back of the head. It is impossible to give up anything if you still believe that what you are removing from your life is a benefit to you. Alcoholics who try and force themselves to stay sober will live in total misery until they relapse, because subconsciously they believe their life is less without the substance they crave. Put an obese individual in a pizza restaurant with their friends all chowing down on pizza whilst they only have a healthy salad and watch as they slowly go out of their mind in agony.

Those physical pathways that have been created in the brain are kept alive not only by completing the routine that they are there to facilitate, but also by the thought of completing the routine. The brain can't tell the difference between a real time event and a vividly imagined version of it. When the legendary golfer Jack Nicklaus was asked how he won the masters so many times and with such apparent ease, he said, 'it's simple, I played the courses hundreds and hundreds of times in my head before I even got to the tee. When I got on the course I just had to do it one more time'.

When you go on a diet your conscious mind demands that you eat less food than you want to eat, your subconscious programming demands the opposite and you create your own personal civil war. The fact that you are now thinking about food more than ever before breathes continual life into the physical pathways that you desperately wish would go away.

Simply put, the only way to give up anything is genuinely not to want it anymore. You simply don't think about things that you don't want. If you are thinking about something then ergo you must care about it, even if you state that you don't. Frequently you will hear people boast about how in control of alcohol they are by saying things like 'I can take it or leave it, sometimes I go months without a drink'. Such statements sound very laudable, but if I change the substance see what happens to the context; 'I can take or leave carrots, sometimes I go months without eating a carrot'. If I made such a claim would you think I had a healthy relationship with carrots or I had a big problem with them?

Presumably you don't need to force yourself to not inject class A street drugs on a daily basis, but why? They are highly addictive and make you feel amazing. Why don't you have to constantly remind yourself not to inject heroin? Because you don't want it and you don't believe it is a benefit to you.

Another good example of the failure of will-power in action is our collective attitude to exercise. I can't tell you how many cold mornings in January I have woken up with the decision to join a gym and get fit right at the top of my mental to do list. I proudly walk into the health club and commit myself to a year-long membership (why wouldn't I, after all, this time I am really going to commit) only to find that my early enthusiasm fades to naught and I have just found another way to dispose of my income every month.

Have you ever driven past a jogger running in the cold and wet and thought 'what and idiot' but at the same time feeling a little guilty that you are driving the half mile to the shop to buy a pint of milk? If someone is lean, fit and out jogging in terrible conditions, the chances are they are not forcing themselves to do anything. Despite what you think, they are enjoying what they are doing,

57

otherwise they wouldn't be doing it, or perhaps more accurately, they wouldn't *keep* doing it.

If the jogger you have observed is an overweight guy, sweating profusely with a facial expression that demonstrates nothing but pure misery, the chances of repeatedly seeing that guy in the act of jogging are somewhere between slim and none. If you want to jog, find a way to really enjoy it, if you hate it you have to use will-power.

Will-power creates unhappiness, and it's the stripping away of this action of the ego that creates peace, creates freedom, creates happiness.

Chapter Five
Principle Three – Flow like the river

Understand that nothing on earth is permanent, absolutely everything is temporary. In the same way that the river may always have been there, the water that allows it to exist is always changing, always different. Life flows like the river and is not about gaining possessions or objects, these are symptoms of the frailty of your conscious mind or ego. Most people believe if a certain set of events were to happen they would finally be happy. If they just got that job they had always wanted… if they could only win the lottery, or if the girl of their dreams would just agree to a date, then life would be perfect. A life based on reaching a destination is doomed to failure because there is no such thing as a final destination. It's about the journey and not the result of it.

The message of this chapter is for you to let go of and forget about the past, it's gone. And stop trying to plan your journey into the future. It's not yours to control and try as you might you will fail to engineer what your ego wants. Remember, the past is history, the future is a mystery, but today is a gift; that's why it's called the present.

Embracing the temporary in everything and accepting that nothing can ever be permanent is truly a blessing, but you are free to waste an entire lifetime finding that out for yourself if you prefer. Animals know this better than us and that is why you never seen animals building permanent structures; homes to live in all their life. Animals don't ever try and own things; they understand that all they have in the current moment is all that matters. The food they had yesterday has gone and trying to predict how much they will have tomorrow is a pointless activity.

As I sit writing this chapter of The Secret Law of Subconscious Attraction, a formation of geese have just flown overhead in a perfect and silent V shaped flight pattern. Whilst the goose at the head of the V has to work considerably harder than the others, he doesn't complain or resent the other members of the group. Instinctively when he tires another goose will silently move into position and allow the tiring animal to move into the less resistant slipstream. If geese had a human ego then they would fall from the sky in a shambolic and violent argument as the lead goose declared how unfair it is that he must shoulder the burden of the increased wind resistance at the front of the V.

Animals are less cursed by the negative effects of the ego and simply flow in the stream of nature. They never try to make themselves more attractive, when was the last time you saw a rabbit styling its hair? Animals just exist in the temporary perfection of life, and there is a profound lesson waiting for you by pausing in the middle of the chaos of your life and observing animals and insects.

Watch a spider build its web, be aware of how in the moment it lives. The spider creates an amazing and intricate construction. Swot away the web and does the spider down tools in temper, throw the towel in and give up, or does it simply start again? Does the spider ever demonstrate anger that you ruined all its hard work, or does it work slower on the second web because it is disappointed to have to repeat the task over again?

No. The spider doesn't care about what went before, it is gone and as only the ego lives in the past and a spider doesn't have an ego, it is of no concern. Neither are concerns of whether that web will still be there tomorrow, without the curse of the ego (the precise thing we in the western world believe makes us superior) nothing exists but the precise moment.

Humans on the other hand are driven by their crazy egos, an insane part of us that constantly demands that we find more and more ways to avoid the inevitable. We are always trying to build our perceived levels of significance by trying to own more and more things. We buy cars, houses, art and other trappings that we can point to and say, look how important I am. The futility of this will become more and more apparent to you the older you get. I know multi-millionaires who are now in what we would describe as the twilight of their lives who would gladly give away every single penny for the chance to be young again. I equally know as many young people who would give up everything for the chance to be rich – youth really is wasted on the young!

One of the best pieces of advice I ever heard is to remember that life is just a piece of theatre and you are one of its actors. Your life and everything in it is just your part in the script. It is not who you really are, and the bad things are not really happening, it's all an illusion. The secret is to strip away the ego that believes you are the character you are playing and see that you are instead the actor enjoying his work hidden beneath the greasepaint and make-up.

If you are struggling to see how you can live like a creature devoid of an ego when you are clearly a human, suffering with that very affliction, I can tell you that for most people there is a point in your life when you will be able to experience that exact state of being. Sadly, when you reach this point you are normally months, weeks or days away from death. When people are diagnosed with terminal illness and after they have allowed the conscious mind to fruitlessly try to push the river back up the stream. When they reach the point where they stop swimming against the stream and let go, they accept the inevitable and a profound and beautiful peace wraps itself around them.

In this moment, when they have accepted and stopped fighting against death, the ego begins to die. In the final days these people experience awareness of life from a purely divine prospective; for the first and last time in their life, they see the truth.

Bronnie Ware is a palliative care nurse who, for many years, worked purely with people who had been sent home to die. The medical profession could do no more for them and the only remaining objective was to ensure a pain-free death in a comfortable and familiar environment. As Bronnie helped these people and got to know them over their final weeks she started to notice that there were some very common threads amongst the things they said of their lives on earth.

Bronnie started to make notes on what these dying people were saying and she realized that there were five main observations that were made by virtually all people who knew they were about to pass away.

1. I wish I'd had the courage to live a life true to myself, not the life others expected of me.
This was the most common regret of all. When people realise that their life is almost over and look back clearly on it, it is easy to see how many dreams have gone unfulfilled. Most people have not honoured even half of their dreams and had to die knowing that it was due to choices they had made, or not made.
It is very important to try and honour at least some of your dreams along the way. From the moment that you lose your health, it is too late. Health brings a freedom very few realise, until they no longer have it.

2. I wish I didn't work so hard.
This came from every male patient that Bronnie nursed. They missed their children's youth and their partner's companionship. Women also spoke of this regret. But as most were from an older generation, many of the female patients had not been breadwinners. All of the men she

nursed deeply regretted spending so much of their lives on the treadmill of a work existence.

By simplifying your lifestyle and making conscious choices along the way, it is possible to not need the income that you think you do. And by creating more space in your life, you become happier and more open to new opportunities, ones more suited to your new lifestyle.

3. I wish I'd had the courage to express my feelings.

Many people suppress their feelings in order to keep peace with others. As a result, they settled for a mediocre existence and never became who they were truly capable of becoming. Many developed illnesses relating to the bitterness and resentment they carried as a result.

We cannot control the reactions of others. However, although people may initially react when you change the way you are by speaking honestly, in the end it raises the relationship to a whole new and healthier level. Either that or it releases the unhealthy relationship from your life. Either way, you win.

4. I wish I had stayed in touch with my friends.

Often they would not truly realise the full benefits of old friends until their dying weeks, and it was not always possible to track them down. Many had become so caught up in their own lives that they had let golden friendships slip by over the years. There were many deep regrets about not giving friendships the time and effort that they deserved. Everyone misses their friends when they are dying.

Try not to beat yourself up; It's common for anyone in a busy lifestyle to let friendships slip. But when you are

64

faced with your approaching death, the physical details of life fall away.

People do want to get their financial affairs in order if possible. But it is not money or status that holds true importance for them; they want to get things in order more for the benefit of those they love. Usually though, they are too ill and weary to ever manage this task. Despite what your ego believes now, it all comes down to love and relationships in the end. That is all that remains in the final weeks, love and relationships.

5. I wish that I had let myself be happier.
This is a surprisingly common one. Many did not realise until the end that happiness is a choice. They had stayed stuck in old patterns and habits. The so-called 'comfort' of familiarity overflowed into their emotions, as well as their physical lives. Fear of change had them pretending to others, and to their selves, that they were content. When deep within, they longed to laugh properly and have silliness in their life again.

You can choose to continue pushing the river up the hill and wait for this knowing to finally arrive into your life, granted at a point where you can't do anything with the knowledge but pass it on to others. Or you can decide to change your life today, to stop kicking and allow the water to carry you to where it wants to take you.

You do this with the knowledge that you are not your thoughts, the real you is eternal. Your ego lives in a state of blind panic because it knows it is essentially a piece of meat inside your head, and one day it will die. Your subconscious is not concerned as it knows that your body is not who you are, it is merely a container for your divine energy while you are here on earth. The ego loves anything that creates the illusion of permanency, not just with bricks and mortar but with people and relationships too.

Actually, principle three is REALLY the most important of all the eight principles of The Secret Law of Subconscious Attraction… To be like the river and feel the peace you need to subconsciously attract the life of your dreams, you must find a way die before your death. Give up everything that can be taken away by death, and in that moment you will find the most perfect state of bliss imaginable. In that moment you will be free, and freedom creates happiness.

The beauty of this secret you are discovering is there is nothing you need to do to become a master of sub-attraction. If anything you just need to lay back on the Lilo and float down the river knowing that you can only end up at source. Your ego will object and insist that it will find a way to swim back up the river, but it is just a deluded little puppy dog falsely believing it is a terrifying beast. The solution comes when you let go of the egoic need to control the uncontrollable and let the universe take over.

I will finish this chapter with a profound story of the thirsty Buddha:

Once Buddha was walking from one town to another with a few of his followers. While they were travelling, they happened to pass a lake. They stopped there and Buddha told one of his disciples, I am thirsty. Do get me some water from that lake there.

The disciple walked up to the lake. When he reached it, he noticed that some people were washing clothes in the water and, right at that moment, a bullock cart started crossing through the lake. As a result, the water became very muddy, very turbid. The disciple thought, how can I give this muddy water to Buddha to drink? So he came back and told Buddha, "the water in there is very muddy. I don't think it is fit to drink".

After about half an hour, again Buddha asked the same disciple to go back to the lake and get him some water to drink. The disciple obediently went back to the lake. This time he found that the lake had absolutely clear water in it. The mud had settled down and the water above it looked fit to be had. So he collected some water in a pot and brought it to Buddha.

Buddha looked at the water, and then he looked up at the disciple and said, "see what you did to make the water clean. You let it be... and the mud settled down on its own and you got clear water... Your mind is also like that. When it is disturbed, just let it be. Give it a little time. It will settle down on its own. You don't have to put in any effort to calm it down. It will happen. It is effortless".

What did Buddha emphasize here? He said, "it is effortless". Having 'peace of mind' is not a strenuous job; it is an effortless process. When there is peace inside you, that peace permeates to the outside. It spreads around you and in the environment, such that people around start feeling that peace and grace.

Chapter Six

Principle Four – Our divine power – The most important principle bar none

Despite what physicality we believe makes us who we are, at our core we are nothing but an invisible source of divine power. The nameless that we insist on naming, an eternal being of no shape, size, depth or any other earthly dimension that you care to think of. Beyond the shell that we call our body, we are a fragment of God lodged within a temporary container.

Your brain is separated into two halves, but they are not equal in size, power or importance. Every second of every day your body is bombarded with millions of pieces of information from the speed of your heart, the temperature of the room, the color of the sky and onwards a million times over. Your conscious mind is capable of being aware of around 10-15 of these pieces of information at any one time with the power to concentrate on just one thing at a time... try it! Try and think of two things at the same time without joining them together somehow. If it suddenly became your conscious responsibility to run your body, to pump your heart and regulate you're breathing, you would be dead within seconds. Thankfully, despite how hard we try to cease control from the subconscious, we will never succeed.

So here is the secret to everything in your life that you don't like. Whether you smoke and hate it, are overweight and will do absolutely everything you can to keep your shameful body covered, are afraid of heights or have an annoying habit of dating people who treat you like dirt. It's all created by your subconscious beliefs, a part of you directly connected to source.

So there really is a bit of us that is God… The problem with the popular interpretations of traditional religions is that they tend to paint the picture that we as mere humans are a constant disappointment to a God who is somehow removed from our world. An old bearded man sitting in the clouds who sometimes listens but often appears to choose not to. It's this viewpoint that creates questions like 'if God exists, how could he let so many bad things happen?' If you consider for a moment that God isn't anywhere specific and isn't separate from us, it changes your opinion on everything. In my book 'The God Engima', I go into detail about why I believe God is not a solus individual. Instead, try to imagine this eternal divine power as an infinite piece of ice that has shattered into billions of pieces and inside every person, animal and object on earth is embedded a sliver of that ice. One day it will melt and return to its source, but for our time on earth it belongs to us. If you can take that leap of faith and accept that God is nowhere but rather a part of us, you can see why when you raise your eyes to heaven and pray for something you want, there is often no reply… God is not where you think it is.

The universe listens to your subconscious and delivers what it says without question. The route of all your problems is along our journey through life; we pick up bad programming. Our subconscious becomes tainted by the ego and outside influences. Think of the worst thing in your life at the moment, whether that is debt, disease, illness, anxiety or loneliness. It's all there because your subconscious believes it should be.

The good news is, if you put it there you must also be able to remove it! True… and using the techniques in this book everything in your life can be changed by erasing the programming and giving the space it occupied back to the universe. Divinity knows exactly what your heart desires and wants to give it to you. But you must create the space or void before it can happen. God begins from zero, a blank canvas that is first filled with love.

The atheist was arguing with the spiritual guru, stating that God did not exist and when we die that's it, there is no heaven, there is nothing. The guru smiled and said "the thing you call nothing, to me is everything".

Everyone has dreams and wishes, and when you become desperate enough you may even turn to prayer. For many in the western world this noble deed doesn't last long as our impatience makes us think our prayers go unanswered. This is not true, every prayer is answered, it's just that sometimes the answer is no, and at other times it is a qualified yes, as in 'not now but later'. When most people drop to their knees and ask God for something and they don't get the response they

71

want, their assumption is that God either did not hear, chose to ignore, or worse still, that God doesn't exist.

God exists within you; he is embedded inside you as that fragment we talked about earlier. That divine inner power comes with the ability to answer your own prayers. That is the only way they will ever get answered, the guy sitting on the cloud isn't there! So this chapter of The Secret Law of Subconscious Attraction is all about the biggest question of all; exactly how do we get our prayers answered and live a life of happiness beyond our wildest dreams?

Riding a bicycle is simple if you know how to do it, right? But when you first tried to get on one and ride, did you not fall flat on your face? Initially you could stay on that thing for more than a couple of seconds before tumbling off and collecting a few cuts and bruises on the way. Eventually your dad probably fitted training wheels to that bike so you wouldn't get discouraged. Once your confidence had grown and more importantly you believed you could ride the bike, he took the stabilizers off and set you on your way with a helping push. Manifesting through prayer is no different; it is a simple thing to do <u>when you know how</u>. The difference is, hardly anyone stops you when you are getting it wrong and puts your training wheels on for a while.

The standard practice for most people when they pray for something specific is to adopt the kneeling position, close their eyes and direct their thoughts upwards to the heavens. They say something like "God, please help me pay the bills this month, we work very hard and when payday comes there is still not enough money to make ends meet. Make this month better than last month and allow something to happen so we have enough to get by. If you can do that for me I promise I will come to church more often / give to charity more / be a better person" etc, etc.

A month later and the bills remain unpaid, the person feels his prayer was ignored and then the ego kicks in again with the usual nonsense of 'God must be punishing me'. Why do we find it easier to assume that God is angry with us than he didn't hear it in the first place? In reality that person answered their own prayer, but they didn't get the outcome they wanted because they placed the request in the future. This person stated that the present moment is bad and the future will be better. Only the ego operates in the past and in the future, the soul and God work only in the present.

You can tell when you are communicating with the ego because of the positioning in time of the statements. If you are talking about what went before, or speculating about what will happen in the future, the conscious mind is active and the subconscious is disengaged. All promises are statements of the ego, even the ones that appear to be well-intentioned. Many will hold marriage up as the counter argument to this point, stating that in this moment of loving union God requires us to make promises of fidelity and commitment to each other.

God did not write the marriage vows, a human did. God requires nothing of you beyond what you are right now in this moment. Marriage, like every other decision, will either serve you or it won't, but don't be under any illusion that those publically made statements are anything other than the ego attempting to control the uncontrollable by predicting the future.

Please don't misunderstand, I am not out to do marriage down, I am married myself and I love my wife and children very much. However, I believe whilst some get a great deal out of marriage and evolve as a soul because of the lessons learnt during the process of sharing a life. Many, many more individuals slowly become resentful and unhappy trying to comply with the needs and desires of another.

If we come to earth as physical beings in order to experience life as a separate entity, why would the logical goal be to settle down with another as soon as we leave the nest? The ego is a huge fan of marriage because it simply adores statements that make promises based on 'forever more'. Your soul knows how you feel about your partner in life right now in this moment, but it will never try to predict that you will feel the same in ten year's time, next week or even in the next minute. Only the ego tries to make predictions of the future based on events of the past, and for that reason all promises are simply statements of the ego.

As you stand at the alter and look into your husband's eyes and promise to love him for the rest of time, you are writing promises your soul can't cash. Who knows how you will feel in a week's time, never mind a lifetime. On your ruby wedding anniversary you may be just as head over heels in love as you were on your wedding day or you may be desperately unhappy. It's impossible to know, but that doesn't stop your ego from trying to convince you that it does know.

Because of this, any prayers set in or reliant upon events of the future are destined to fail because they are only statements and desires of the ego and nothing more. Prayers are answered by your soul, the fragment of God operating in blissful ignorance of the past and future concerned only with the now.

Ask your soul for a lottery win this weekend and you will get nothing in return. You are not being denied the money that you no doubt desperately need, but rather it is impossible for your wish to be granted because the approaching weekend does not exist in the eyes of your soul. The only thing that exists from the point of view of God is the precise moment in which you offer the prayer up. The only effective prayer is one of gratitude for the money you have in that precise moment. To become a creator of your destiny rather than someone who reacts to the life that has been forced upon them, you need to see the beauty in every moment and be grateful for it.

Think about this moment now, what is amazing in your life now? If your automatic answer is 'nothing, my life sucks at the moment', you are not trying hard enough.

Spend a few moments thinking about what is really special in your life now.

Let me give you an example of how you can choose to focus on the negative and incorrectly make your prayers based on that. At the moment I know that I feel sad because I don't get to see my family enough because my work takes me around the world. I feel guilty that I don't get to be the father that I dreamt I would be because I am away on business so often. I know there is big tax demand on the way and I am not looking forward to paying that... I could go on and on. Then I could drop to my knees and say 'God, please let me spend more time with my family and help me pay the tax demand' etc, etc. I will tell you now that prayer will not work, or perhaps more accurately, I should say that prayer would not give me the outcome I desire.

All that prayer will deliver is more of what I have focused on at the time. In that precise moment I had 'sadness', 'guilt' and 'worry' on offer, and that is exactly what I will get more of as a result. Your soul is a divine creator, a manifestation weapon of limitless power, but with the safety switch off... be careful where you point that thing, it might go off! Aim it at the negative and it will create more negatives (free will is a pain right?), but aim it at the positive and guess what happens?

So let's talk about me again (my ego will love this), but instead of thinking about the lack of time I got to spend at home last month, or that big bill that is coming next month, let's stay in this precise moment and build a prayer based on that.

Right now I am so grateful that I am sharing this knowledge with you, I know that these words resonate with me at a very deep level and I am excited about the impact they might make to kindred spirits around the world. I have two stunningly amazing children who I love with all my heart. My wife Denise is my rock back at home, she always has a smile and a welcome for me when I return home, and she is there whenever I need someone I can trust (I could pick up the phone and speak to her right now if I so desired). I have food, shelter, safety and all the other basic requirements of life. It's 7.15am and I am sat at my desk listening to the soft summer rain outside, today is a blank canvas and I am grateful for the world of opportunities available to me.

Wow, suddenly I feel good... I really encourage you to do the same task, and do it now. Don't let your ego make a promise that you will do this later, grab a piece of paper and start writing now. Scribble down all the amazing things in your life, ignore the stuff that has gone before and avoid the shoulda, woulda, coulda's.

And here is the final but most magical piece of information for this chapter; how to get your prayers answered every time... Be the outcome you desire, it really is as simple as that. Want to be wealthy? Then act wealthy, be grateful for the wealth that you have, even if you have nothing but a few coins in your pocket, be grateful for them. Instead of thinking about yesterday when you had more coins or predicting that by tomorrow you will have none at all. Stay in the moment of now, and love the fact that you have money.

Act like you have money, I don't mean go waste it on desires of your ego, but give it away if the Primary Thought Events tells you that's what you should do. When you give away something the subconscious assumes you must have plenty, and so it works to create that reality. Who would have thought that giving away money creates more money? Hey, and you know what, it works with everything; want more love? Then give more love! But remember that (free will) safety switch is always turned off, give away abuse and negativity and guess what your life gets more of?

By the way, there is nothing wrong with wanting more money as long as you always remember that money is just an idea and nothing more. What we believe money to be is actually nothing of the sort. The currency in our pocket is nothing more than an I.O.U, the money in your bank account is nothing more than numbers on a screen. Because money is a made up concept, you can have as much as you imagine you should have.

Some say that money makes the world go round, whilst that's not strictly true and the world would continue quite happily without the concept of money, cash does flow and circulate like blood coursing around a body, and if you stop that natural momentum of wealth by hoarding what you have, by acting like Scrooge you prevent more of what you crave flowing into your life. It sounds illogical at first, but in reality the giving of money creates a multi-level subconscious portal to open. The amount you give away (without expecting anything back in return) is relative to the size hole it creates in the attraction field. Through this vortex, like water surging through a plug hole and into the awaiting drainpipe, money returns.

The secondary level benefit of this proven law of attraction is subliminal damage to what Stephen Covey calls the scarcity mindset. Your subconscious cannot tell the difference between reality and a vividly imagined event. So whether you are wealthy or just believe you are wealthy is all the same thing at an unconscious level. Logically, therefore if you are freely giving away money to worthy causes that have touched your heart or inspired you somehow, then you simply cannot be afraid to lose money and money cannot be a scarce resource.

Most people who attempt a will-power based diet will at some point stall in their progress as their subconscious protection systems become aware that food appears to be in limited supply. The body switches to starvation mode to hang on to the very thing you want to lose, that big wobbly belly! The exact same principle applies to your finances, if your mind switches into scarcity mode for anything, you can be assured you will get nothing but everything you don't want. Scarcity mode prevents the flow of money by attempting to dam the river and stockpile what you have. This prevents the flow of money from entering your life.

Of course, there is a danger hidden within the words of this book. What I write here with good intentions to encourage you to find peace can just as easily be interrupted by your ego as an excuse to ride rough shot over other people's feelings on a new 'permitted' journey to find pleasure. So far I have told you that the rules of other people create misery, bad and good don't really exist, and you should let go and forgive yourself of your past mistakes. In the egoic mind of an unawakened soul, this could appear to be a license to do pretty much anything you feel like doing, regardless of the impact it has on others.

The easily made error is to confuse pleasure with happiness. Happiness comes from within, not from without, and does not require any external element to be present. Pleasure is only the shadow that happiness casts against the wall. Pleasure is so shallow that it can be generated purely from the respite of misery. If you were chained to the wall in a foreign jail cell and cruel prison guards tortured you for hours on end. When they stopped, whilst you would still be in pain the level will have dropped and it's this improvement that many people assume is happiness.

If you are 100% unhappy with your life because you are overweight, in a job you hate, poor or lonely, then suddenly the situation changes as a result of some good fortune and you win a small amount on the lottery, which pays off a few bills but not enough to allow you to quit your job. Your level of measured unhappiness is now 80%. By experiencing the drop from 100 to 80 you assume you have discovered happiness, the money made you happy, right? Wrong! You are still 80% unhappy.

On the 12th July 1964, Nelson Mandela stood before a judge and jury charged with an array of politically motivated crimes against the state. He summed up his defense by saying "During my lifetime I have dedicated myself to the struggle of the African people. I have fought against white domination, and I have fought against black domination. I have cherished the ideal of a democratic and free society in which all persons live together in harmony and with equal opportunities. It is an ideal which I hope to live for and to achieve. But if needs be, it is an ideal for which I am prepared to die".

With that moving statement he was promptly sentenced to life imprisonment and spent the next 27 years locked in a tiny cell on his own.

Meet Nelson Mandela today and he is one of the most optimistic, smiling, contented and happy of men you will ever meet. How? Mandela was dealt a hand so much more severe and unfair than the one most of us got. After nearly three decades in solitary confinement how is he not a broken shell of a man?

Nelson Mandela understood that people can persecute you, hurt you and cage you away from the light of day but they can never extinguish the perfect flame that burns within you. To keep that flame alive all you must do is be aware of it.

Happiness is within, and pleasure is always without. The delusion of the ego is that it incorrectly believes it can take pleasure and convert it into happiness. This is like trying to make an omelet out of a photograph of some eggs. It appears you have the right ingredients but pleasure is just no more real than the reflection of yourself in the mirror is real.

A luxurious piece of chocolate cake with butter cream icing tastes amazing at first and gives you intense pleasure, but what happens if you follow your ego and try to make that pleasure permanent by continuing to eat slice after slice of that rich cake? All you have done is repeat the thing that created pleasure, but now you feel the opposite, you feel sick and uncomfortable. Suddenly the thing you believed was pleasurable now doesn't taste very good at all.

A clear indicator of when you are obeying the commands of your ego is when you pursue more of something. Your ego can never be satisfied and will always demand more of everything it believes will generate pleasure.

When you open a bottle of fine wine and take that first sip, allowing the rich and flavorsome liquid to tingle over your palate and swamp your taste buds with its intoxicating taste. Why don't you put the bottle away having experienced the pleasure you initially craved? Why is it necessary to pour a second glass? Is it not true that the second glass doesn't quite taste as good as the first? And how good does the tenth glass of that wine taste?

Pleasure is the shadow cast on the wall by happiness, but no matter how many shadow puppets you make at no point will they become real. Trying to make pleasure permanent is like filling a leaking barrel of water with a bucket. You will spend a lifetime not quite getting anywhere.

Whenever you want more of something it is nothing but your ego making a demand, and this applies to everything. If you believe that more money will make you happy, you are being lied to by yourself. If you think more love is all you need to feel content, you will find that there is simply not enough love in the world to ever satisfy you. Even if you believe that all that is wrong with your life is you need more sex and passion, you will find that there is never quite enough to tick the box.

This does not mean you shouldn't partake in pleasurable things, you should do what you feel you need to do, but be aware you are satisfying needs of the ego and nothing more. Your thinking mind can be distracted and amused with the most simple and basic of acts. I am almost certain you have laughed at the sight of someone else falling over in the past, is another person's accident really pleasurable, or is it the ego's delight that the misfortune didn't happen to you the real source of the amusement.

The German's even have a name for this black humor. 'Schadenfreude' is defined as pleasure derived from the misfortunes of others. Surely we have all at some point taken pleasure from the misfortune of others?

When I worked as a late night radio presenter for a commercial radio station in the North West of the United Kingdom I would have to prepare for my nightly broadcast in a shared open plan office. Another local radio station in our company had their studios in the same building. One Monday night the usual guy didn't show up and instead a new presenter called Tony, who had been given the competing show to mine on our sister station, walked through the door. I greeted him and showed him where the coffee machine was located, almost as essential as oxygen to us late night guys!

As I showed him around and made polite small talk he stopped and looked me straight in the eye and snarled 'I am going to wipe the floor with you'. I was quite taken aback, I had never considered the other station a threat to me as we were both focusing on completely different audience demographics. I was on a young contemporary hit music station and he was on an AM talk format.

"You are going to regret the day I walked into this place, I am coming after all your audience and when I am finished with you there will be no doubt as to who is cutting it at this time of day in this patch", he continued with some seriously unnecessary venom in his words.

Our relationship never really got any better than that and far from cause me a problem, he continued to struggle in the ratings for nearly eighteen months. Until the station he worked for approached me and asked me to come over to their side not only as a broadcaster but as the manager of the station. My brief was to improve the audience figures, and it was very clear who was first to go in the big overhaul of the brand.

I called Tony in and as professionally and politely as I could I informed him that we were not renewing his contract and parting company. He broke down in tears, emptied his locker into a plastic bag and headed for the door. Did it upset me, firing Tony? No, not really. In fact, I will admit a little dark side of me thought it couldn't have happened to a nicer guy, and I was almost glad it was my finger on the trigger. But did it make me happy? No.

Pleasure is part of why we choose to experience life in physical form, but to be happy you should be able to strip away all pleasure and still feel content. Pleasure is sedation for the ego, and having a human ego is similar to carrying around with you a priceless crystal glass. You can show the glass off and revel in the attention that it brings, you can fill the glass with fine wine, but the price you pay for carrying this delicate and precious article around with you is that it can be very easily damaged or smashed by others. Happiness is different because it resides protected within, enveloped by your soul and untouchable by anyone but you.

Chapter Seven
Principle Five – Ho'oponopono Everything

Now if you thought the other principles were important, let me tell you they have nothing on Principle Five! Ho'oponopono is the ancient Hawaiian spiritual process of acceptance, forgiveness and gratitude. Rosario Montenegro offers one of the most concise stories of how Dr Hew Len brought this amazing tradition into popular modern culture around the world.

More than thirty years ago, in Hawaii, at the Hawaii State Hospital, there was a special ward, a clinic for the mentally ill criminals. People who had committed extremely serious crimes were assigned there either because they had a very deep mental disorder or because they needed to be checked to see if they were sane enough to stand trial. They had committed murder, rape, kidnapping or other such crimes. According to a nurse that worked there in those years, the place was so bleak that not even the paint could stick to the walls; everything was decaying, terrifying, repulsive. No day would pass without a patient-inmate attacking another inmate or a member of the staff.

The people working there were so frightened that they would walk close to the walls if they saw an inmate coming their way in a corridor, even though they were all shackled, all the time. The inmates would never be brought outside to get fresh air because of their relentlessly threatening attitude. The scarcity of staff was a chronic occurrence. Nurses, wardens, and employees would prefer to be on sick-leave most of the time in order not to confront such a depressive and dangerous environment.

One day, a newly appointed clinical psychologist, a Dr. Stanley Hew Len, arrived at the ward. The nurses rolled their eyes, bracing themselves for one more guy that was going to bug them with new theories and proposals to fix the horrid situation, who would walk away as soon as things became unpleasant, around a month later, usually. However, this new doctor wouldn't do anything like that. Actually, he didn't seem to be doing anything in particular, except just coming in and always being cheerful and smiling, in a very natural, relaxed way. He wasn't even particularly early in arriving every morning. From time to time he would ask for the files of the inmates.

He never tried to see them personally, though. Apparently he just sat in an office, looked at their files, and to members of the staff who showed an interest he would tell them about a weird thing called Ho'oponopono. Little by little things started to change in the hospital. One day somebody would try again to paint those walls and they actually stayed painted, making the environment more palatable. The gardens started being taken care of, some tennis courts were repaired and some prisoners that up until then would never be allowed to go outside started playing tennis with the staff. Other prisoners would be allowed out of their shackles, or would receive less heavy pharmacological drugs. More and more obtained permission to go outside, unshackled, without causing trouble to the hospital's employees.

In the end, the atmosphere changed so much that the staff was not on sick leave any more. Actually, more people than were needed now go to work there.

Prisoners gradually started to be released. Dr. Hew Len worked there close to four years. In the end, there remained only a couple of inmates that were eventually relocated elsewhere, and the clinic for the mentally insane criminals had to close.

Simply put, Ho'oponopono is based on the knowledge that anything that happens to you or that you perceive, the entire world where you live is your own creation and thus, it is entirely your responsibility.

Your boss is a tyrant? It's your responsibility. Your children are not good students? It's your responsibility. There are wars and you feel bad because you are a good person, a pacifist? The war is your responsibility. You see that children around the world are hungry and malnourished if not starving? Their want is your responsibility. No exceptions. Literally, the world is your world, it is your creation. As Dr. Hew Len points out: didn't you notice that whenever you experience a problem, you are there?

It's your responsibility, doesn't mean it's your fault, it means that you are responsible for healing yourself in order to heal whatever or whoever it is that appears to you as a problem.

It might sound crazy, or just plain metaphorical, that the world is your creation. But if you look carefully, you will realize that whatever you call the world and perceive as the world is your world, it is the projection of your own mind.

If you go to a party you can see how in the same place, with the same light, the same people, the same food, drink, music and atmosphere, some will enjoy themselves while others will be bored, some will be overenthusiastic and some depressed, some will be talkative and others will be silent.

The "out there" for every one of them seems the same, but if one were to connect their brains to machines, immediately it would show how different areas of the brain would come alive, how different perceptions there are from one person to the next. So even if they apparently share it, the "out there" is not the same for them, let alone their inner world, their emotions.

How do you heal yourself with Ho'oponopono? Three steps: by recognizing that whatever comes to you is your creation, the outcome of bad memories buried in your mind; by regretting whatever errors of body, speech and mind caused those bad memories, and by requesting divine Intelligence within yourself to release those memories, to set you free. Then, of course, you say thank you.

There are seminars where they teach you many tricks to help this process, but according to Joe Vitale, Dr. Hew Len himself uses the simplest of the formulas from Ho'oponopono. Whenever a matter arises –and they arise incessantly– addressing the Divine within you, you only have to say: I'm sorry, Please forgive me, Thank You, I Love you.

If you want to discover more about the origins and evidence of Ho'oponopono, look out for a book by Joe Vitale called Zero Limits. Joe goes into great detail about how this amazing principle that has been passed down the ages literally creates miracles.

What you will discover if you download one of my subconscious reprogramming tracks is that there are distinct traces of this method running through every recording. Whilst you will rarely hear me make reference to Ho'oponopono, you will most certainly hear me use the words 'I am sorry, please forgive me, thank you and I love you' throughout the hypnosis tracks.

Whether you are just trying to stop smoking or are looking to attract the person of your dreams into your life you will find a subattraction ™ download that targets your precise desire or problem via the website at craigbeck.com

For this important step of the eight principles of the Secret Law of Subconscious Attraction you must simply accept your imperfection and seek forgiveness for it. I absolutely do not mean you need to apologize in the Catholic confessional sense of the word, heaping a gigantic load of shame on your own shoulders. This guilt achieves nothing, your acceptance and apology is simply a way of stating that you understand there is something manmade within you that is preventing divinity flowing. God/Source/The Universe is not disappointed, annoyed or ashamed of you, as all those emotions are purely human states and not relevant to a perfect source of

90

creation. You cannot clear the bad programming or erroneous beliefs in your subconscious with your conscious mind.

Only the universe can clean the misaligned patterns and it's through this apology that you allow the process to begin. You are completely unaware of what beliefs are hidden and so you can't even begin to find them. Just accept that they are there, that they are your complete responsibility and you are sorry for their very existence. Ask the universe, source, divinity, God or whatever you want to call it, to forgive you and your bad programming. Ask for it to be erased and replaced with nothing, a void that can be filled with the pure white light of divinity.

As you begin this process you will start to feel that your life is like a vase full of water, when the container is empty of joy and love, you feel disconnected from source. When the vase is full to the brim the contents soon go stale like a stagnant pond. To achieve perfection in life the contents of the vase must continually be flowing. As you empty that vase of love into other people's lives it creates space for more love to flow in.

Create the space daily for more love to flow into your life by giving away as much as you can, there will always be an abundance if you have the space to receive what is waiting and willing to come into your life.

As you consider becoming the vessel for the pure white light of the universe, and finally for this chapter of the Secret Law of Subconscious Attraction, let me tell you the story of The Universe's own branch of Starbucks.

A group of alumni, highly established in their careers, got together to visit their old university professor. Conversation soon turned into complaints about stress in work and life.

Offering his guests coffee, the professor went to the kitchen and returned with a large pot of coffee and an assortment of cups – some were chipped and broken, some porcelain, plastic, glass, crystal, some plain looking, some expensive, some exquisite - telling them to help themselves to the coffee.

When all the students had a cup of coffee in hand, the professor said:

"If you noticed, all the nice looking expensive cups were taken up, leaving behind the plain and cheap ones. While it is normal for you to want only the best for yourselves, that is the source of your problems and stress.

Be assured that the cup itself adds no quality to the coffee. In most cases it is just more expensive and in some cases even hides what we drink.

What all of you really wanted was coffee, not the cup, but you consciously went for the best cups... And then you began eyeing each other's cups.

Now consider this: Life is the coffee; the jobs, money and position in society are the cups. They are just tools to hold and contain Life, and the type of cup we have does not define, nor change the quality of life we live.

Sometimes, by concentrating only on the cup, we fail to enjoy the coffee God has provided us."

The universe brews the coffee, not the cups... Enjoy your coffee!

Chapter Eight
Principle Six - Have an attitude of gratitude

So here at number six of eight we move onto the most important principle of the Secret Law of Subconscious Attraction. Have an attitude of gratitude. A popular and perhaps over-pronounced statement, but one that is rarely used selflessly. Many people who first come into contact with the Law of Attraction hear that in order to attract something you want, you must act like you already have it. To give thanks as though that new car or lottery win is already in your possession.

As we have already discovered; your conscious desires and wants are an irrelevance, so forget about what you think you want. These dreams are all in the tomorrow and none of your business. Concentrate on what is in your life today, this moment, and be grateful for it. Even problems present as an opportunity for love and gratitude. Give your problems to God, ask God to erase them and then give thanks for that.

I think Marelisa Fabrega describes it best in her change blog when she says:

Gratitude means thankfulness, counting your blessings, noticing simple pleasures, and acknowledging everything that you receive. It means learning to live your life as if everything were a miracle, and being aware on a continuous basis of how much you've been given.

Gratitude shifts your focus from what your life lacks to the abundance that is already present. In addition, behavioural and psychological research has shown surprising life improvements that can stem from the practice of gratitude. Giving thanks makes people happier and more resilient, it strengthens relationships, it improves health, and it reduces stress.

Two psychologists, Michael McCollough of Southern Methodist University in Dallas, Texas, and Robert Emmons of the University of California at Davis, wrote an article about an experiment they conducted on gratitude and its impact on well-being. The study split several hundred people into three different groups and all of the participants were asked to keep daily diaries. The first group kept a diary of the events that occurred during the day without being told specifically to write about either good or bad things; the second group was told to record their unpleasant experiences; and the last group was instructed to make a daily list of things for which they were grateful. The results of the study indicated that daily gratitude exercises resulted in higher reported levels of alertness, enthusiasm, determination, optimism, and energy. In addition, those in the **gratitude** group experienced less depression and stress, were more likely to help others, exercised more regularly, and made greater progress toward achieving personal goals.

People tend to take for granted the good that is already present in their lives. There's a gratitude exercise that instructs that you should imagine losing some of the things that you take for granted, such as your home, your ability to see or hear, your ability to walk, or anything that currently gives you comfort. Then imagine getting each of these things back, one by one, and consider how grateful you would be for each and every one. In addition, you need to start finding joy in the small things instead of holding out for big achievements—such as getting the promotion, having a comfortable nest egg saved up, getting married, having the baby, and so on–before allowing yourself to feel gratitude and joy.

Another way to use giving thanks to appreciate life more fully is to use gratitude to help you put things in their proper perspective. When things don't go your way, remember that every difficulty carries within it the seeds of an equal or greater benefit. In the face of adversity ask yourself: "What's good about this?", "What can I learn from this?", and "How can I benefit from this?"

Once you become oriented toward looking for things to be grateful for, you will find that you begin to appreciate simple pleasures and things that you previously took for granted. Gratitude should not be just a reaction to getting what you want, but an all-the-time gratitude, the kind where you notice the little things and where you constantly look for the good, even in unpleasant situations. Today, start bringing gratitude to your experiences, instead of waiting for a positive experience in order to feel grateful; in this way, you'll be on your way toward becoming a master of gratitude.

If you want to read more about the theories of gratitude, check out some more of the fantastic blogs from Marelisa online.

If you live the eight principles of the Secret Law of Subconscious Attraction for the next 21 days, I guarantee you will start to witness miracles. Start right now; be grateful for everything in your life right now in this moment. Keep a gratitude journal on your desk or by your bed. Start and end each day with a huge list of how wonderful your life is and you will be amazed at what happens.

I don't just need you to do this in the good times, but it is even more important that you do it in the dark times. When life doesn't seem worth living, when you are down on your luck, pick up the pen and be grateful for the good things.

I tell you nothing here that I don't do myself and I will admit that I am no saint and I do have to wear a reminder to ensure that I constantly live in a state of gratitude for my life in this moment. I have never found wearing jewelry comfortable and so I don't own any necklaces, rings or other decorative adornments, I don't even wear a watch for the same reason. However, around my left wrist I do wear a simple cotton string. It is there for one reason, when I look at it, I automatically say the words, 'everything in this moment is perfect'.

When I finally give up playing the character 'Craig Beck' and give up on this body and shuffle off the stage, I think they should engrave my tombstone with 'Everything in this moment is just perfect!'

The ego will always disagree with the sentiment of this principle, but it will also always be wrong, as is clearly demonstrated in the wonderful story of the American Dream:

An American businessman was standing at the pier of a small coastal Mexican village when a small boat with just one fisherman docked. Inside the small boat were several large yellow fin tuna. The American complimented the Mexican on the quality of his fish.
"How long did it take you to catch them?" the American asked.
"Only a little while," the Mexican replied.
"Why don't you stay out longer and catch more fish?" the American then asked.
"I have enough to support my family's immediate needs," the Mexican said.
"But," the American then asked, "What do you do with the rest of your time?"
The Mexican fisherman said: "I sleep late, fish a little, play with my children, take a siesta with my wife, Maria, stroll into the village each evening where I sip wine and play guitar with my amigos. I have a full and busy life, senor."
The American scoffed: "I am a Harvard MBA and could help you. You should spend more time fishing and with the proceeds you could buy a bigger boat and, with the proceeds from the bigger boat, you could buy several boats. Eventually you would have a fleet of fishing boats. Instead of selling your catch to a middleman, you would sell directly to the consumers, eventually opening your own factory. You would control the product, processing

and distribution. You would need to leave this small coastal fishing village and move to Mexico City, then LA and eventually NYC where you will run your expanding enterprise."

The Mexican fisherman asked: "But senor, how long will all this take?"

To which the American replied: "15-20 years."

"But what then, senor?"

The American laughed and said: "That's the best part. When the time is right, you would announce an IPO - an Initial Public Offering - and sell your company stock to the public and become very rich. You would make millions."

"Millions, senor? Then what?"

The American said slowly: "Then you would retire. Move to a small coastal fishing village where you would sleep late, fish a little, play with your kids, take a siesta with your wife, stroll to the village in the evenings where you could sip wine and play your guitar with your amigos..."

Chapter Nine
Principle Seven - Time is an illusion that you don't control.

Time, as we know it, is only an illusion. We usually think of time as having three parts - Past, Present, and Future. But what is the Past - only a collection of memories. We can't experience the Past, we can only remember it. And we can only remember it in the Present (furthermore, our memories are noticeably unreliable). There is no objective thing that we call the Past; it can't be measured in any way; our only contact with it is in the Present.
And what is the Future - only a mental construct in the Present. We can't experience the Future until it "becomes" the Present. Until then it is only a hope and dream. We can project what the Future may be like, but we are considerably less accurate than when we remember the Past. There is no objective thing that we call the Future; it can't be measured in any way; our only contact with it is in the Present.
That leaves us with the Present - **the ever changing Present**. Actually, if you want to be true to yourself about time, you should wear a watch that simply says 'now', but you may pretty quickly establish a reputation for being late.

It's actually the impatience of the ego that creates the compelling arguments that our prayers are not answered. If you subconsciously believe in something, it will happen, that much is automatic and there is nothing that can stop it happening. The frustration for us to accept is that we don't really know when is best for that thing to arrive. However, the universe absolutely does, and your dream will be delivered at the precise moment when it is best for you to experience it. Your prayer is answered in the perfect moment it was always intended to be, not a second before or after that point.

What we must accept is that to flow like the river we must arrive at the sea when the river dictates, and not when we believe we should be there. The law of attraction is as similar to the genie in the lamp story as it is poles apart from it. You really can manifest anything and everything you desire, but it is not as simple as rubbing a dirty lamp and finding your dreams appear before you in a flash of light and a puff of white smoke. So, before you start dreaming and praying for all the things you believe you need to be happy, ask yourself the question 'is everything not perfect just as it is?' There is an old saying that goes 'be careful what you wish for', and let me tell you why that is very true.

Many years ago I dreamed that my words would reach thousands of people just like you. I thought the principles I was starting to live my life by could help many, many other people around the world given the chance to hear them. As a slight aside to the point I will tell you that I am probably most proud of my work on alcohol addiction because I believe there are millions of hard working people drinking a bottle of wine a night under the illusion that they are normal (because it's also what their friends do) and they are not addicted to a powerful and deceptive drug. I struggled with alcohol for nearly seventeen years until I changed the way I subconsciously felt about the act of drinking, and then, as if by magic, one day I just stopped and for good, I did it without pain or will-power.

Despite having tried to quit many times before, this time I just knew I would never drink again. That is how you can tell the switch has been flicked in the opposite direction. When you don't just 'think it' but you actually 'know it', at that point you don't have to fight or swim furiously up the stream. Suddenly the water appears to be flowing exactly to where you want to go and you can relax and float along with the current, what you desire will just appear exactly as the water will always reach the ocean. I don't ever crave a drink and even in the middle of a party where everyone is chugging back the booze, the last thing I want to do is join them.

I promise I am heading back to the point I was about to make, but if you are interested to know more about my method to stop drinking then I strongly urge you to download my audiobook ' Alcohol Lied To Me'.

'Be careful what you wish for' they say, and with good reason. I didn't just think I wanted my work to be published and released to the world, I knew it was going to happen. There was never a fragment of doubt in my mind, body or soul. I flicked the switch and passed a command to the universe, it was going to be delivered to me no matter what happened. Obviously, my ego insisted that it arrived immediately if not sooner. I was sure I was ready and I enthusiastically sent my first two books to dozens of carefully researched publishers.

Over the following six months a slow tide of rejection letters landed in my mailbox. I didn't expect it to be a walk in the park and so I prepared the manuscripts for my second book and sent another giant batch of proposals. Again another half a year passed and my mailbox again filled with polite rejections. I had such unshakable faith in what I was writing I was absolutely dumbstruck by the lack of interest.

I was just about to start on my third blitz to the publishing houses when my life hit a major roadblock. Even as I sit here now I am struggling to think of the words to sum up how bad my life became for a period of nine months. It felt like my whole world came crashing down around me. Everything, and I really do mean everything, that could go wrong did exactly that.
It started with my company losing its main contract with a radio station in the North East of England. This probably accounted for 75% of my income and it was gone over the course of a disastrous meeting one Friday morning at the company HQ. Next, my son started to have a problem with bullying at his school and as a result was coming home in tears virtually every day. As I tried to reassure him in the midst of the financial disaster I had to deal with urgently, my wife Denise fell seriously ill and at times I worried I might lose her.

I would dearly love to report that was the end of our misfortune for that year. One by one another plate that had been previously spinning perfectly started to wobble and fall off. All my investments crashed and became less than worthless overnight. I went from being relatively well off to being close to bankrupt in the space of three months. I had borrowed heavily to create a property portfolio and one at a time I watched each one lose more and more value every month until I got to the point where I owed nearly a million dollars, and if I sold everything I owned I would still owe nearly half that amount.

I eventually managed to replace the missing income but it would mean I would be away from home 80% of my life. I would need to travel around the world to replace what I had previously got from one local location. This new situation brought my marriage to its knees and I found myself waking up feeling like I was a failure who had let his children down, had no option but to declare bankruptcy and was on a direct track to the divorce courts.

For the next three months I awoke each morning and thought 'what's the point?' and 'why carry on?' What I forgot is that even the most dramatic of thunderstorms come to an end. There has never been an earthquake that has lasted forever. What we know Lao Tzu was trying to tell us 2500 years ago is that everything is temporary and hidden within the dark clouds is the clear sky waiting to break through.

Only when I reached the point where I could no longer summon the energy to continue swimming up the river and gave in. Finally accepting that even in the worst case scenario everything would still be just perfect, then things started to change. What I mean by that is that I reached an acceptance that the river is going to come down the mountain whether I wanted it to or not. If I had to lose everything I had ever worked to attain, if I had to go bankrupt and if my marriage failed, then it was okay. I figured I would still have what is in my head, I would still be who I am as a person, my wonderful children would still call me dad and I would still be free to start all over again on another exciting a fantastic journey.

Early in this book you read about discovering the freedom of dying before your death. To disconnect yourself from everything that you can't take with you when you die. I didn't realize it at the time but this is what I managed to achieve, I found myself in a place where none of the material possessions I had previously cared about really seemed to matter anymore. My accountant tried to drum into me how serious my situation was and he sat there completely bemused by how lightly I appeared to be taking his words. I had already accepted that it would all go, it would all be taken away from me and suddenly it stopped hurting.

As the people I really care about in my life continued to run around with their arms in the air declaring the end of the world is nigh, I calmly sat down at my computer and began to rewrite my first two books. The God Enigma (which was originally called Fragments of God) and Swallow the Happy Pill.

Today I have over twenty published books; the New Science of Persuasion & Influence topped the UK business books chart in 2011. 'The Hypnotic Salesman' was the number one business book in the US, UK and Australia this year and made it to number four on the top one hundred audiobooks sold in the world! Thousands of people have stopped drinking because of 'Alcohol Lied to me' and my inbox is never empty as a result of all the amazing people who I get to interact with on a daily basis as a result of my work.

Here is the point of the rags to riches story… only the universe knows what needs to happen in order for your dreams to become reality. That is why I tell you to be careful what you wish for. There is no way on earth I would have chosen the path I have been on. However, I am immensely grateful for it because I am only who I am now because of that entire trauma I went through during that dark period in my life. The massive pain I experienced in my every waking moment changed me so profoundly that it forced me to approach everything differently. I rewrote the books and I submitted them to just one publisher, the rest, they say, is history.

So as we sit in the middle of one of life's storms wondering why our prayers are being ignored, be assured that the storm is actually the byproduct of your prayers being answered, and in that moment you are sitting on the workbench of God, being crafted and chiseled into the person you long to be. The pain you experience in the dark times is the same pain the carbon feels as it is squeezed and compressed into a beautiful diamond.

The most stunning, precious stones have all been polished to perfection by the harshest and most violent storms nature can throw at them. You are no different, and so I encourage you to stop trying to accelerate time in the bad times and slow it down in the good. Embrace the hard periods of life because they simply mean great things are on the way. Remember, people don't ride rollercoasters for the slow trundle up the inclines, they accept the tedious journey up to enjoy the thrilling ride down.

As this is the most important of the eight principles, it's vital you learn that time is an illusion that you don't control.

Chapter Ten
Principle Eight - Love is everything.

As I am sure you are aware, I have declared each one of the seven principles so far to be the most important. You may be wondering if I am going to be at least consistent with my apparent error and declare principle eight to be the most important too... Love is everything. This principle may not be the most important, but it's just as important as the other seven. Actually, each principle becomes the most important for the period in which we discuss it. As it slips into the past or remains just a principle we will talk about at some point in the future, it remains the speculation of the ego. As with everything else in life, the only thing that matters is what is happening in the now. Life happens in this precise moment, and that applies most definitely to love. The fact that you gave love to someone yesterday and you might very well intended to spread that joy is all irrelevant. The only love that counts is the love you give right now.

From the Tao Te Ching: Assuming that there is a creative force in the universe, that creative force exists and is far beyond human ability to describe in full. Thus, it is the Nameless, and from that Nameless the entire universe (Heaven and Earth) was created.
When we give it a name (God, Buddha, Christ, Zeus, the Great Mystery, etc.) we are trying to put a human face on the Nameless. This causes major differences to appear.

To Christians, the Nameless is really a male God. To Wiccans, there is both a God and a Goddess. Yet, if there is an actual Creative Force, then whatever it is, is far, far beyond human. We try to define the Nameless as male, as female, or as some of both, yet even that reflects our way of thinking for humanity comes in two sexes; male and female.

But the Nameless might have a hundred sexes, or no sex. We try to make something more familiar and easier to handle in our minds by giving it a name. Thus, when we are describing the universe around us, and its creation, we are using the Named, not the Nameless. This is sort of like Plato's parable of the cave; the shadows on the cave wall only represent whatever is really causing the shadows; the shadows are not the things themselves.

If it helps you to understand the concept of God better, replace the label God with the word love. If, when you think of God you still picture the old bearded guy in the clouds. See how it changes things when you rename him as the emotion 'love'... would we still raise our eyes to the heavens, shake our fist and question why 'love' caused the earthquake? If a child were to be born with a terrible disability would we blame 'love' for the genetic mistake?

Remember, everything in your life is your responsibility; your subconscious requested that it be delivered. So to respond to hatred (that you created) with hatred is futile. To become depressed at the state of your bank account achieves and changes nothing. Be prepared to see that only love or 'God' can replace everything bad. As you are indeed a fragment of God – do not look to others to improve your life; it is entirely your task to start.

The thought of sending love to your enemy feels uncomfortable and every flicker of your human emotions tells you not to do it. To instead send them what they deserve, or what you believe they deserve. This is purely the work of the ego; the part of your brain that still believes it can control all. In reality it controls only the initiation of problems in your life. All negative input into your world is caused by the absence of love and thus cannot be fixed by removing more of it. To fix anything in life that is out of balance with the intentions of the divine, you must smother it in love.

These are the eight principles of the core of Subconscious Attraction and the beginning of true awakenings within your soul. I understand that at this stage some may seem far-fetched and nonsensical to you, as they did to me when I first discovered them. So for now, I am asking you to take a leap of faith and for the next 21 days take them as being 100% true (you have nothing to lose). During this time, select an audio download to address your biggest burning desire from the range of mp3's available online at subattraction.com. Load the audio onto your audio player and find a quiet, darkened room where you can listen every day for at least 21 days. The tracks are designed to fit in around busy lifestyles and never last longer than 15 minutes.

Don't lie there waiting for something magical to happen, don't expect or demand anything – you are not in control and neither am I. Just relax and let the music and my words drift over you. It's fine if you find your mind wandering or even if you drift off to sleep. There is nothing that you can do wrong, free yourself of that concern and let go of all expectation. If it helps, focus on what you believe divinity looks like. For some it's nothing, just a sea of infinite darkness, for others it is pure white light that swirls and flows around them. It doesn't matter what you decide it looks like, as long as your intention is true.

Thank you for reading the "The Secret Law of Attraction' with me, I sincerely hope the material in here changes your life to the extent that it has changed mine. If this book has made the impact I dreamed it would then you have made me eternally happy. I recommend you start from the beginning and read the whole thing over again, because something magical happens when you read it again blessed with the full knowledge of what is to come.

If you have any questions or want to share your story with me, please contact me via the website at www.CraigBeck.com

As a final favor to me, if you have enjoyed this book please take a few moments to return to the online store you bought it from and rate and review it… it always means a lot to me.

Remember, your subconscious is capable of limitless power; literally anything you desire can be yours if you believe yourself worthy of it. Not just consciously but by allowing that positive energy to flow unrestricted into your unconscious image of who you believe you really are. Today is the day you flick the switch.

Recommended links
- http://www.CraigBeck.com
- http://www.StopDrinkingExpert.com

Manifesting Magic Coaching Program

Do you want to be the next person to start living the life of their dreams?

Life is harsh right? But if you work long and hard you can ease the struggle… no pain, no gain!

Wrong, wrong, wrong! Virtually everything you have been told about how to have a happy, successful life is wrong. Not just a little bit wrong but the exact polar opposite of the truth!

So many people spend an entire lifetime not quite having enough… they get stuck in a job they don't like, in a relationship that isn't healthy and struggle along always with not quite enough money.

Life is not meant to be a struggle, money is not supposed to be scarce and you are not here to spend half your precious time on this planet working in a job that doesn't fulfill you and leaves you wondering what the point of it all is!

- *Yes I know you read 'The Secret' & it didn't work the way you hoped.*
- *Yes I know you tried positive thinking & found it impossible to maintain.*
- *Yes I know you have read self-help books & a hundred other things.*

Why didn't any of that work & why don't you have the life you dream of?

The truth has been sanitized to appeal to a mass market – remember, what I am about to show you flies in the face of what virtually everyone currently believes. Only a very select few people will be open minded enough to be able to process this knowledge.

I do not advertise this website... Most people never find this coaching program, there is a reason you are here. You should trust me on this because a uniquely magical experience is just a mouse click away. Why not decide now and join my Manifesting Magic Coaching Program today?

I want you to be the next person whose life completely changes beyond their wildest dreams.

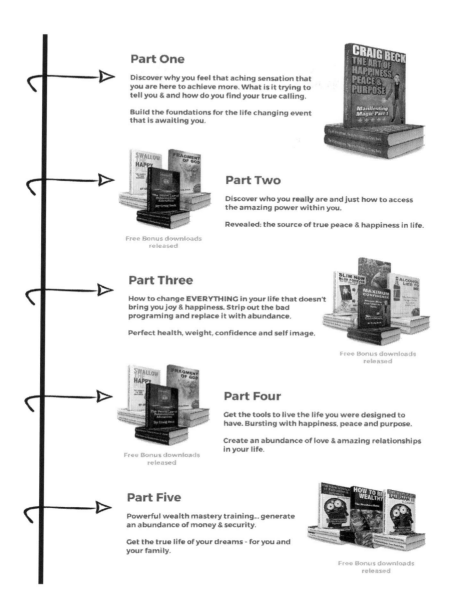

Part One

Discover why you feel that aching sensation that you are here to achieve more. What is it trying to tell you & and how do you find your true calling.

Build the foundations for the life changing event that is awaiting you.

Part Two

Discover who you really are and just how to access the amazing power within you.

Revealed: the source of true peace & happiness in life.

Free Bonus downloads released

Part Three

How to change EVERYTHING in your life that doesn't bring you joy & happiness. Strip out the bad programing and replace it with abundance.

Perfect health, weight, confidence and self image.

Free Bonus downloads released

Part Four

Get the tools to live the life you were designed to have. Bursting with happiness, peace and purpose.

Create an abundance of love & amazing relationships in your life.

Free Bonus downloads released

Part Five

Powerful wealth mastery training... generate an abundance of money & security.

Get the true life of your dreams - for you and your family.

Free Bonus downloads released

www.CraigBeck.com

23708142R00071

Printed in Great Britain
by Amazon